[H.A.S.C. No. 113–105]

# RUSSIAN MILITARY DEVELOPMENTS AND STRATEGIC IMPLICATIONS

————

## COMMITTEE ON ARMED SERVICES
## HOUSE OF REPRESENTATIVES

### ONE HUNDRED THIRTEENTH CONGRESS

SECOND SESSION

————

HEARING HELD
APRIL 8, 2014

————

U.S. GOVERNMENT PRINTING OFFICE

88–450          WASHINGTON : 2015

For sale by the Superintendent of Documents, U.S. Government Printing Office,
http://bookstore.gpo.gov. For more information, contact the GPO Customer Contact Center,
U.S. Government Printing Office. Phone 202–512–1800, or 866–512–1800 (toll-free). E-mail, gpo@custhelp.com.

# COMMITTEE ON ARMED SERVICES

## ONE HUNDRED THIRTEENTH CONGRESS

### HOWARD P. "BUCK" McKEON, California, *Chairman*

MAC THORNBERRY, Texas
WALTER B. JONES, North Carolina
J. RANDY FORBES, Virginia
JEFF MILLER, Florida
JOE WILSON, South Carolina
FRANK A. LoBIONDO, New Jersey
ROB BISHOP, Utah
MICHAEL R. TURNER, Ohio
JOHN KLINE, Minnesota
MIKE ROGERS, Alabama
TRENT FRANKS, Arizona
BILL SHUSTER, Pennsylvania
K. MICHAEL CONAWAY, Texas
DOUG LAMBORN, Colorado
ROBERT J. WITTMAN, Virginia
DUNCAN HUNTER, California
JOHN FLEMING, Louisiana
MIKE COFFMAN, Colorado
E. SCOTT RIGELL, Virginia
CHRISTOPHER P. GIBSON, New York
VICKY HARTZLER, Missouri
JOSEPH J. HECK, Nevada
JON RUNYAN, New Jersey
AUSTIN SCOTT, Georgia
STEVEN M. PALAZZO, Mississippi
MO BROOKS, Alabama
RICHARD B. NUGENT, Florida
KRISTI L. NOEM, South Dakota
PAUL COOK, California
JIM BRIDENSTINE, Oklahoma
BRAD R. WENSTRUP, Ohio
JACKIE WALORSKI, Indiana
BRADLEY BYRNE, Alabama

ADAM SMITH, Washington
LORETTA SANCHEZ, California
MIKE McINTYRE, North Carolina
ROBERT A. BRADY, Pennsylvania
SUSAN A. DAVIS, California
JAMES R. LANGEVIN, Rhode Island
RICK LARSEN, Washington
JIM COOPER, Tennessee
MADELEINE Z. BORDALLO, Guam
JOE COURTNEY, Connecticut
DAVID LOEBSACK, Iowa
NIKI TSONGAS, Massachusetts
JOHN GARAMENDI, California
HENRY C. "HANK" JOHNSON, JR., Georgia
COLLEEN W. HANABUSA, Hawaii
JACKIE SPEIER, California
RON BARBER, Arizona
ANDRE CARSON, Indiana
CAROL SHEA-PORTER, New Hampshire
DANIEL B. MAFFEI, New York
DEREK KILMER, Washington
JOAQUIN CASTRO, Texas
TAMMY DUCKWORTH, Illinois
SCOTT H. PETERS, California
WILLIAM L. ENYART, Illinois
PETE P. GALLEGO, Texas
MARC A. VEASEY, Texas
TULSI GABBARD, Hawaii

ROBERT L. SIMMONS II, *Staff Director*
KIMBERLY SHAW, *Professional Staff Member*
MICHAEL CASEY, *Professional Staff Member*
AARON FALK, *Clerk*

(II)

# CONTENTS

---

## CHRONOLOGICAL LIST OF HEARINGS

### 2014

---

## TUESDAY, APRIL 8, 2014

## RUSSIAN MILITARY DEVELOPMENTS AND STRATEGIC IMPLICATIONS

### STATEMENTS PRESENTED BY MEMBERS OF CONGRESS

### WITNESSES

### APPENDIX

# RUSSIAN MILITARY DEVELOPMENTS AND STRATEGIC IMPLICATIONS

---

HOUSE OF REPRESENTATIVES,
COMMITTEE ON ARMED SERVICES,
*Washington, DC, Tuesday, April 8, 2014.*

The committee met, pursuant to call, at 10:03 a.m., in room 2118, Rayburn House Office Building, Hon. Howard P. "Buck" McKeon (chairman of the committee) presiding.

## OPENING STATEMENT OF HON. HOWARD P. "BUCK" MCKEON, A REPRESENTATIVE FROM CALIFORNIA, CHAIRMAN, COMMITTEE ON ARMED SERVICES

The CHAIRMAN. The committee will come to order. Good morning, ladies and gentlemen.

The committee meets to receive testimony on "Russian Military Developments and Strategic Implications." Immediately following this hearing, Members will receive a classified briefing by representatives from our intelligence community.

Joining us today are Assistant Secretary of Defense for International Security Affairs Derek Chollet and Joint Staff Director for Strategic Plans and Policy Vice Admiral Frank Pandolfe.

Thank you both for being here today and for your service to our Nation.

Before we get started, I would like to welcome Congresswoman Tulsi Gabbard to the committee. Congresswoman Gabbard brings a wealth of experience and unique perspective, having served our Nation as an enlisted soldier and officer. With Tulsi and Colleen Hanabusa, the service men and women of the U.S. Pacific Command and in the great State of Hawaii are well represented.

We look forward to working with you.

The events unfolding in Ukraine are deeply troubling, from Russia's invasion and occupation of a sovereign country to its amassing of tens of thousands of troops along Ukraine's borders and further north under the ruse of conducting snap exercises. Just this past weekend, we saw reports that Russia is provoking further unrest in eastern Ukraine, attempting to create a reason to invade.

Yet these actions are only the most recent and perhaps most aggressive of a broader campaign to challenge the West and to reestablish a Russian sphere of influence in Europe.

Mr. Putin is directing a multidimensional military modernization effort. Russia is re-arming at an alarming rate, with military spending up roughly 30 percent. It stands in flagrant violation of a major nuclear arms control treaty and, under the New START [Strategic Arms Reduction Treaty] Treaty, is building up its nuclear forces by over 100 warheads since the last declaration, while the U.S. reduces its own forces.

As former Secretary of Defense Robert Gates recently wrote in an op-ed, and I quote, ''Mr. Putin is playing a long game, and the West must also play a strategic long game. Yet the administration's policies have rested largely on reset, cooperation, and further nuclear cuts.''

Just last week, Deputy Under Secretary Christine Wormuth, testifying on the QDR [Quadrennial Defense Review], stated that they ''probably would have added some additional sentences about Russia, given recent developments.'' That is hardly a reexamination of our Nation's policy towards Moscow.

And while the QDR states that our military is sized to and capable of effectively deterring aggression, there are serious concerns about our ability to do just that, especially with a near-peer competitor.

Our friends, as well as our adversaries, are watching our every move. It should come as no surprise that senior Japanese officials raised this issue with Secretary Hagel during his recent visit, as they seek to understand what our policy with regard to Russia's illegal annexation of Crimea signals for our commitments to our allies.

This hearing is an opportunity to examine the strategic implications of Russia's military developments and recent actions. Secretary Chollet and Admiral Pandolfe, I hope you can also discuss how these developments are influencing any reexamination of U.S. policy towards Russia, including our force posture in Europe, how we reassure our allies and partners, and our defense investments.

Gentlemen, thank you for appearing before our committee, and I look forward to your testimony.

Mr. Smith.

[The prepared statement of Mr. McKeon can be found in the Appendix on page 41.]

### STATEMENT OF HON. ADAM SMITH, A REPRESENTATIVE FROM WASHINGTON, RANKING MEMBER, COMMITTEE ON ARMED SERVICES

Mr. SMITH. Thank you, Mr. Chairman. I, too, welcome our witnesses today, look forward to their testimony and their expertise on this issue.

And I want to join you in welcoming Congresswoman Gabbard to the committee. It is great to have her here. Obviously, Hawaii is a critical piece of our national security strategy and Department of Defense activities in Asia and beyond, so it is great to have that expertise there. And with her, I believe, 11 years of service, now as a captain in the Army National Guard, her service in Iraq, I think that expertise is going to serve the committee very, very well.

And I thank you for being here. Welcome to the committee.

This is an incredibly important hearing, as we try to confront the challenges that the chairman, I think, described very well. What Russia has done in the Ukraine is a blatant violation of international law, a blatant violation of all manner of different treaties which Russia has signed, and is something that we in the U.S. and I believe every other nation in the world must do all we can to discourage and to send the message that it won't be tolerated and that type of behavior is outside of the international norm.

Because it can potentially lead to destabilization in many places. If it becomes accepted that you can simply decide to take over another country and annex parts of them, it does not contribute to the international order.

Now, this is a difficult situation. It is easy to say that we should not tolerate that; much more difficult to do. I don't think anybody on this committee wants to go to war with Russia over the Ukraine. But we do want to find a way to stop them from further aggression. And I think there are options.

And, overall, this is a very unfortunate choice that President Putin has made, and it is not in the best interests of Russia. Once the Soviet Union collapsed, there was a real opportunity for Russia to move in and become one of the partner of nations, a great power that could participate with other great powers in building a more peaceful, prosperous, and stable world. They had that option.

President Putin has chosen not to take that. He has chosen to further isolate Russia and find further conflict. I think this is a huge mistake. We have already seen the impact on the Russian economy. If Russia had been more willing to embrace the West and work with us, I think it would have led to greater economic opportunity and greater prosperity.

The Russian population is in a very bad place right now. They have an aging population; they have an economy that is in trouble, rampant with corruption. It is not going to help them, to further destabilize their very own region and further turn the international community against them.

I very much agree with President Obama, who said these actions by Putin are more a sign of weakness than they are a sign of strength. The question is, what do we do in response? I think initially we have to take whatever steps we can to try and economically isolate them. We have begun that process; I think we should continue it.

But key to all of this will be NATO [North Atlantic Treaty Organization] and the EU [European Union]. Whatever amount of business we do with Russia, whatever our economic leverage over Russia is, the EU has at least 10 times that. They can make decisions to show Russia that this type of behavior won't be tolerated much more easily than we can.

So I am very interested to hear from our witnesses about what our best approach is to working with our partners in Europe and to get full-scale cooperation in not just condemning Russia's actions but to make them pay a price for it that will make them think that this is not in their best interests.

This is not easy. Regrettably, in many, many countries throughout the world, we have found that we cannot simply force them to behave in ways that we would like them to. But we have to try to alter this behavior, certainly condemn it, but try to find ways to hopefully make sure it does not happen in the future and to defuse the ongoing situation in the Ukraine. There is continuing concern that it will spread beyond Crimea into the eastern Ukraine and become even more of a problem.

So, very curious to hear from our witnesses today about how we can contain that and respond to the Russian aggression in the Ukraine in a way that will not make the situation worse but hopefully will change Putin's calculations in the future.

With that, I yield back and look forward to the testimony of the witnesses.

[The prepared statement of Mr. Smith can be found in the Appendix on page 43.]

The CHAIRMAN. Thank you.

Mr. Secretary.

### STATEMENT OF HON. DEREK CHOLLET, ASSISTANT SECRETARY OF DEFENSE FOR INTERNATIONAL SECURITY AFFAIRS, OFFICE OF THE SECRETARY OF DEFENSE FOR POLICY, U.S. DEPARTMENT OF DEFENSE

Secretary CHOLLET. Thank you, Mr. Chairman, thank you, Congressman Smith, members of the committee, for this hearing today. I very much appreciate the opportunity to speak with you on U.S. policy and actions in the wake of Russia's incursion in the Ukraine and how the Department of Defense has worked with our allies and international partners to address this issue.

Russia's unlawful military intervention against Ukraine challenges our vision of a Europe whole, free, and at peace. It changes Europe's security landscape, it causes instability on NATO's borders, and it is a challenge to the international order.

Since the outset of this crisis, the United States has pursued three courses of action: first, demonstrating support to Ukraine's transitional government; second, reassuring allies and deterring Russia from further military threats to Europe; and third, imposing costs on Russia for its illegal actions.

The Department of Defense has an important role in achieving these objectives in all three areas. First, to support Ukraine, the United States has worked with partners like the IMF [International Monetary Fund], the U.N. [United Nations], the EU, the G–7 [Group of Seven], to provide Ukraine with political backing and economic assistance, including an $18 billion package from the IMF.

For our part, the Department of Defense is working with Ukraine to review, prioritize, and grant its defense assistance requests for materials and supplies that would serve to support Ukraine without taking actions that would escalate this crisis militarily.

The initial round of this process was completed last week, with the delivery of 300,000 MREs [meals ready-to-eat] to support Ukrainian forces in the field. This is the support that they had asked for. We have maintained senior-level defense dialogues with Ukrainian counterparts throughout this crisis. And we have led efforts at NATO to offer Ukraine greater access to NATO exercises, invite Ukraine to participate in the development of military capabilities, and provide capacity-building programs to the Ukrainian military.

The second course of action is reassuring U.S. allies and deterring Russia from further military action in Europe. As President Obama said recently during his trip to Brussels and his meeting with the NATO Secretary General there, the NATO alliance is, quote, ''the bedrock of America's security as well as European security.'' And just last week, NATO celebrated its 65th anniversary.

Reassurance measures so far include augmenting NATO's peacetime Baltic air policing mission; deploying air assets and personnel to Poland to supplement the U.S.-Poland aviation detachment, or AVDET, training rotation; and extending the USS *Truxtun* stay in the Black Sea to conduct exercises with Romanian and Bulgarian naval forces. We will also send another ship to the Black Sea within a week.

NATO has also established orbits of Airborne Warning and Control System, or AWACS, aircraft over Poland and Romania, both to serve as additional assurance to allies that border Ukraine and to enhance NATO's situational awareness of activities in the region.

The third course of action is imposing costs on Russia. Russia's violations of its own agreements and international law require a vigorous, coordinated response, and the United States has led the international community in isolating Russia diplomatically.

Along with the European Union, Canada, and Australia, the U.S. has imposed visa restrictions and comprehensive sanctions on a growing list of Russian officials, one Russian bank, and members of Putin's inner circle, along with Ukrainians who played a role in undermining that country's sovereignty and misappropriating Ukrainian assets. As the President has made clear, the sanctions we have imposed to date are not the end of what we can do.

At the Department of Defense, we have put on hold all military-to-military engagements with Russia, including exercises, bilateral meetings, port visits, and planning conferences. Although we have worked hard over two decades to try to build a cooperative, transparent defense relationship with Russia, the violations of international law and the undermining of stability in Europe mean that we cannot proceed with business as usual.

NATO and many allies have likewise suspended military cooperation engagements with Russia, while maintaining the channels for dialogue that can serve to deescalate this crisis. And while we do not seek military confrontation with Russia, its actions in Europe and Eurasia may require the United States to reexamine our force posture in Europe and our requirement for future deployments, exercises, and training in the region.

Mr. Chairman, Congressman Smith, members of the committee, let me conclude by saying that Russia's unlawful actions in Ukraine have dire implications for international and regional security. This has caused a paradigm shift in our relations with Moscow. And this crisis is not one that has been generated by the West or the United States; it is a crisis of choice pursued by Russia to further what I believe is a distorted view of its own interests, which will only lead to its further isolation.

Finally, I want to thank the Congress for passing the Support for the Sovereignty, Integrity, Democracy, and Economic Stability of Ukraine Act of 2014. This act is closely aligned with the Administration's objectives. It demonstrates solidarity with Ukraine, helps to reassure our allies, and imposes further costs on Russia for its actions.

Since the stakes are high and the international principles are so fundamental, it is important that the United States speak with one voice during this crisis, and I appreciate that we are doing so.

Thank you very much, Mr. Chairman, and I look forward to your questions.

[The prepared statement of Secretary Chollet can be found in the Appendix on page 45.]

The CHAIRMAN. Thank you.

Vice Admiral.

### STATEMENT OF VADM FRANK C. PANDOLFE, USN, DIRECTOR FOR STRATEGIC PLANS AND POLICY (J–5), JOINT STAFF, U.S. DEPARTMENT OF DEFENSE

Admiral PANDOLFE. Good morning, Chairman McKeon, Ranking Member Smith, and distinguished committee members. Good morning, and thank you for this opportunity to update you on Russian military developments.

You just heard a review of actions taken by the United States, the NATO alliance, and the international community in response to Russia's unlawful military intervention in Ukraine. Russia's seizure of Crimea is a flagrant violation of international law, and it reintroduces into Europe the threat of external aggression. By doing so, Russia has set back decades of international progress.

The United States military and the wider NATO alliance have supported our response to this unwarranted intervention. We have given support to Ukraine by way of material assistance, defense consultations, and the offer of enhanced training. We are reassuring our NATO allies, with whom we have Article 5 security guarantees, by sending additional air power to the Baltic States and Poland, increasing our surveillance over Poland and Romania, and sending naval ships into the Black Sea.

And we are helping to impose costs on Russia by halting all bilateral military-to-military interaction. However, as noted by Mr. Chollet, we are keeping open channels for senior-leader communications to help deescalate the crisis.

I now would like to widen the focus of my remarks beyond Ukraine to discuss the evolution of Russian conventional military power, thereby providing context to today's events.

At the height of its military power, the Soviet Union was truly a global competitor. With millions of people under arms, vast numbers of tanks and planes, a global navy, and an extensive intelligence-gathering infrastructure, the Soviet military machine posed a very real and dangerous threat.

Following the breakup of the Soviet Union in 1991, that arsenal fell into disrepair. Starved of funding and fragmented, Russian military capabilities decayed throughout the 1990s.

From the start of his term in office in 2000, President Putin made military modernization a top priority of the Russian Government. When Russia invaded Georgia in 2008, a number of shortcomings were noted in its military performance. This led the Russian Government to further increase investment in its military services.

Since 2008, those efforts have had some success. Russian military forces have been streamlined into smaller, more mobile units.

Their overall readiness has improved, and their most elite units are well-trained and equipped.

They now employ a more sophisticated approach to joint warfare. Their military has implemented organizational change, creating regional commands within Russia. These coordinate and synchronize planning, joint service integration, force movement, intelligence support, and the tactical employment of units.

Finally, the Russian military adopted doctrinal change, placing greater emphasis on speed of movement, the use of special operations forces, and information and cyber warfare. As noted, they instituted snap exercises. These no-notice drills serve the dual purpose of sharpening military readiness while also inducing strategic uncertainty as to whether they will swiftly transition from training to offensive operations.

Today, Russia is a regional power that can project force into nearby states, but it has very limited global power projection capability. It has a military of uneven readiness. While some units are well-trained, most are less so. It suffers from corruption, and its logistical capabilities are limited. Aging equipment and infrastructure, fiscal challenges, and demographic and social problems will continue to hamper reform efforts.

The United States, in contrast, employs a military of global reach and engagement. The readiness of our rotationally deployed forces is high, and we are working to address readiness shortfalls at home.

And we operate within alliances, the strongest of which is NATO. Composed of 28 nations, NATO is the most successful military alliance in history. Should Russia undertake an armed attack against any NATO state, it will find that our commitment to collective defense is immediate and unwavering.

Russia's military objectives are difficult to predict, but it is clear that Russia is sustaining a significant military force on Ukraine's eastern border. This is deeply troubling to all states in the region and beyond, and we are watching Russian military movements very carefully.

I spoke with General Breedlove, the Commander of U.S. European Command and NATO's Supreme Allied Commander, last Friday. He is formulating recommendations for presentation to the North Atlantic Council on April 15th. These recommendations will be aimed at further reassuring our NATO allies. As part of this effort, he will consider increasing military exercises, forward-deploying additional military equipment and personnel, and increasing our naval, air, and ground presence. And he will update Members of Congress on those recommendations at the earliest opportunity.

Ladies and gentlemen, thank you for this opportunity to address your committee. I look forward to your questions.

[The prepared statement of Admiral Pandolfe can be found in the Appendix on page 51.]

The CHAIRMAN. Thank you.

Secretary Chollet and Admiral Pandolfe, as I mentioned in our opening statement, at our QDR hearing last week, Deputy Under Secretary Wormuth commented that, in light of recent events, they would have added some additional sentences on Russia in the

QDR. I would think that a more comprehensive policy review is necessary.

Can you please describe specific steps that the Department is taking to reexamine U.S. policy towards Russia and our posture in Europe? Additionally, what immediate steps is the Department taking to provide assistance to Ukraine to reassure other allies and partners in the region and to deter further Russian aggression?

Secretary CHOLLET. Mr. Chairman, I will begin.

As I mentioned in my opening statement, we have taken some very important steps immediately for our NATO partners, with the Baltic air policing mission, which is adding 6 F–15s, and then also the 12 F–16s to the Polish aviation detachment, which has been very warmly welcomed in both Poland and in the Balts, as well.

We have also been in very close touch with our Ukrainian colleagues. And this goes back to when this crisis was first unfolding earlier this year, when Secretary Hagel had multiple phone calls with the Ukrainian Defense Minister at the time, at that point urging the Defense Minister not to get involved in the Ukrainian crisis. And to the Ukrainian military's great credit, they did not get involved in the crisis as it was unfolding.

Since then, we have worked very closely with the Ukrainians to try to understand their needs and to try to address those as quickly as possible. So there was a team in Kiev last week, a team from the Department of Defense as well as EUCOM [U.S. European Command] representation, what is called the Bilateral Defense Commission, to meet with Ukraine to talk with them about their urgent needs but also the strategy that they are seeking moving forward.

And we are working through some of those requests, as I mentioned in my opening statement. We have worked through what they saw as the most urgent, which is to get them some MREs, because their forces have been in the field for a very long time and need those supplies.

In terms of your question, sir, about the QDR, it wouldn't surprise you to hear that I concur with my colleague's comments that she made last week to this committee. We clearly would have changed some of the tone, perhaps, of the QDR, given what has transpired over the last several weeks and Russia's egregious violation of international law.

That said, I think the fundamental strategy of the QDR still holds. And things like the commitment to maintaining a strong technological edge, the importance and the reaffirmation of the transatlantic alliance and working with our strong partners, the commitment to build partner capacity and institute policies to pursue that objective, those are all things that we were doing before this crisis and we are going to certainly continue to do in the days ahead.

And then, finally, as Admiral Pandolfe mentioned, General Breedlove has been tasked by the North Atlantic Council [NAC], NATO's governing body, to come up with a variety of new ideas about ways that we may reassure our NATO allies moving forward, and those are things that he is working through right now. And he is due to present those to the NAC—and then, as the Admiral said, as soon as possible to you—next week.

Admiral PANDOLFE. Sir, I would agree with what Mr. Chollet says.

The process of assessing our relationship with Russia is ongoing. We continually review our strategic relationships within the Pentagon as a matter of course, quite frankly, every year, as we build the next set of plans, the next set of budgets, the next set of strategy documents.

And, clearly, the actions the Russians have taken, described I think quite accurately as a paradigm shift, are causing us to look very hard at some of the assumptions which underlay the planning and prescriptions of the past.

And not just in the United States, either. NATO is undertaking a very similar process of assessing where the Russians are going and where we will go as a collective alliance with the Russians in the future.

The CHAIRMAN. Vice Admiral, you said in your statement, "Today Russia is a regional power that can project force into nearby states but has very limited global power projection capability." I think that is basically the same words the President used last week.

By your definition, what would be a power or a nation—what nation would you consider has power to project, the ability to project power globally?

Admiral PANDOLFE. Well, sir, one important caveat is my statement was focusing on conventional Russian military power. I think it is important to note that the Russian nuclear arsenal is intercontinental in reach and does have, at that level of the employment of force, extreme range.

Regarding the employment of conventional military power on a global scale, I would argue that the United States is really unique in our ability to operate globally. And that is largely a function of the alliances of which I spoke. We have the support, in terms of basing and cooperative training and operations, of a host of other nations who share our values and our vision for the international order.

And not just our military technologies or people, but that systems of alliances and basing is what really allows the Western forces, with the United States at the center, to operate on a global scale.

The CHAIRMAN. So the United States would be the only country that, take away nuclear capability, has the ability to operate globally?

Admiral PANDOLFE. Again, I would think, on a regular basis, on a routine basis, in a significant level of force, I think that is an accurate statement, sir.

The CHAIRMAN. How many ships do we have in our Navy right now?

Admiral PANDOLFE. Well, last time I checked, it was 287. I am not exactly sure what it is today.

The CHAIRMAN. And how many does Russia have?

Admiral PANDOLFE. I would have to go back and check that, sir.

The CHAIRMAN. I saw something last week that they had 300 ships just in the Black Sea.

Admiral PANDOLFE. Well, numbers of ships is certainly one factor, but you also, as you well know, sir, have to look at the tonnage of the ships, the capabilities of the ship, whether they are ocean-going global ships or whether they are, quite frankly, littoral, regional ships with much shorter ranges and capabilities that are geared towards shorter-range missions.

The United States Navy today really is unique in its ability to operate globally and project power globally.

The CHAIRMAN. Can you get that number back to us on the record, how many ships, comparing apples to apples, Russians have compared to our Navy?

Admiral PANDOLFE. Yes, sir.

[The information referred to is classified and retained in the committee files.]

The CHAIRMAN. Thank you very much.

Admiral PANDOLFE. Yes, sir.

The CHAIRMAN. Mr. Smith.

Mr. SMITH. Thank you, Mr. Chairman.

As we look at the specifics of the crisis right now, how would you assess the risk of Russia going further into the Ukraine, most likely, obviously, into the eastern Ukraine? That is where they have amassed troops, where we have heard in recent days that there are Russian nationalists within Ukraine that have seized government buildings and, you know, committed other actions. What do you think the calculation is?

Because, obviously, the next escalation of this crisis would involve that. And that, I mean, certainly there is the long-term, you know, how do we build our relationship with Russia, how do we contain, you know, any global threat. But right now, you know, keeping the crisis from spreading is all about keeping them out of the eastern Ukraine.

You know, how do you see the likelihood of Russia making that decision? And what can we and our allies do to try to discourage that action?

Secretary CHOLLET. Well, Congressman, I know we have a closed session later, and our intelligence colleagues can perhaps provide a little more granularity.

But what I would say to that is we are very concerned about Russia's buildup on Ukraine's eastern border. We have been very clear at all levels of our government, from the President on down, that this is a worrying development and that we want to see Russia deescalate and move forces out of that area.

The events of the weekend, as you mentioned, have been very concerning. As the White House said yesterday, there is strong evidence that some of the actions taking place inside Ukraine, the folks were perhaps paid by the Russians. These aren't spontaneous demonstrations, we believe. And a move into eastern Ukraine would clearly be a very serious escalation of this crisis.

Mr. SMITH. What do we do?

Secretary CHOLLET. So, what we can do. Well, first, at every opportunity we have, we are—including yesterday Secretary Kerry talked to Foreign Minister Lavrov again—making clear that their behavior is unacceptable and that there will be consequences for their actions. We have shown that there already have been consequences for the actions they have taken, and there are more to come if they were to continue along this course.

So punishing Russia is clearly one avenue. The second is to reassure our partners and allies. We have been very clear, the President when he was in Europe several weeks ago made this very clear, our commitment to Article 5, NATO's collective defense commitment, is ironclad. And we are not just saying that, we are trying to demonstrate through our actions, whether it is the Baltic air policing or the Polish aviation rotation, that we mean what we say along those lines.

So this is a very delicate situation. It is very concerning. I don't want to try to sugarcoat it at all, because Russia has a tremendous amount of capability right now deployed on Ukraine's border. And we are watching it very, very closely.

Mr. SMITH. Let's say—just one final question, because most of the questions I have would be better for the classified session.

Let's say that Russia goes into the eastern Ukraine. In essence, we wind up, you know—Ukraine winds up probably being split in half, or some things that are somewhat similar, although on a grander and more problematic scale than what happened in Georgia in 2008, where you have two provinces that are now effectively part of Russia. Now you have a situation where you would have a much larger country, effectively, part of that. What do you think Putin's long-term vision is beyond that?

I know we are very concerned—I met with a consul from Lithuania back in Seattle over the past week. You know, they are very concerned about what Russia would do there. What do you think Russia—because, obviously, it is a whole different step when you go into a NATO country. I mean, that would basically mean war.

Do you think Putin understands that and would be limited to the Ukraine? Do you think there is a risk that there are other places? And are there other places, other than the Baltic nations, that Russia may have designs on that we need to be worried about?

Secretary CHOLLET. Well, sir, I always hesitate to try to put myself in Putin's head, but what I can say is that Russia's behavior clearly seems to be motivated by a sense—and I believe it is a distorted view of their own interests—that they are better off having client states around them that are completely beholden to Moscow.

We don't have that view. We believe that it is up to the countries around Russia itself to decide their own destiny. Russia clearly has interests, legitimate interests, in its neighborhood, but the way it is seeking to pursue those interests is deeply counterproductive, I believe, to what I think is its own interests, but also a clear violation of international law and absolutely unacceptable.

So how far this goes, I don't want to speculate. That is why what we are doing is to make very clear to Mr. Putin and to his entire leadership that their behavior is unacceptable, their actions are unacceptable, and that there will be consequences for actions they have already taken or any further actions they may take.

Mr. SMITH. What are the most important consequences, do you think, that would show that Russia is paying a price for this that we have taken or will take?

Secretary CHOLLET. I think, sir, the main are economic. And that is why we have focused so much on the sanctions initially. The Russian economy is distorted, itself, mainly through petrochemicals. And we have both tried to target particular individuals, obviously, but also the President now, through Executive order, has the ability to look at sectoral sanctions.

Now, as he said in his statement about 2 weeks ago on this subject, when we get into that neighborhood of actions, those are things that could affect us. And we want to be sure that we are smart about the way forward and that we aim before we shoot when it comes to sanctions. But I think, clearly, that is the pressure point that will have the greatest effect on Russian perceptions.

Mr. SMITH. Thank you.

I yield back.

The CHAIRMAN. Thank you.

Mr. Thornberry.

Mr. THORNBERRY. Thank you, Mr. Chairman.

Admiral, I want to pursue, kind of, what the chairman was talking about: how big a deal this is, essentially.

And your responsibility is plans and policies for the Department of Defense across the whole world. I think most people assume that we didn't really have to worry much about a European war anymore, that the economic integration had made that a thing of the past.

You answered the chairman saying something about a paradigm shift, at least with our relations to Russia. But can you expound a little bit about how big a change this is or is not, related to our national security interests when you look at it worldwide? How big a paradigm shift is this for us?

Admiral PANDOLFE. Well, this is a big deal. I mean, the presumption of our relationship with Russia in the post——

The CHAIRMAN. Admiral, can you speak right into the microphone, please?

Admiral PANDOLFE. I said this is a big deal. The presumption of our relationship with Russia, the foundation of our relationship with Russia, was that they were a cooperative, emerging power that was buying into the international order, to include the laws which govern behavior within the integrated economic and legal system.

Their actions, both in Georgia and most recently in Crimea, have clearly indicated that they have limits to the degree to which they are willing to accede those rules. And they are challenging the international order, which most nations rely on for their security and for their prosperity.

So, clearly, it is a paradigm shift, as the words have been used by a number of leaders. And to Chairman McKeon's point, we are reassessing the way forward with the Russians.

I do think, however, we have to keep it in global perspective, as well. As noted, Russia is an important country and it is a regional power, but we have other interests throughout the world which we also must continue to pay attention to. And we must balance our energies to maintain security and stability not just in Europe but in the Middle East and the Far East, as well. And, quite frankly, I think, working with our allies, that is exactly what we are doing.

Mr. THORNBERRY. But wouldn't you also agree that, in those other parts of the world, they are watching to see what happens here, how we handle this? So if you are North Korea or Iran or China, you are watching to see how the United States responds to this Russian incursion. And the potential is that those other places in the world are going to get more dangerous, not less, if they think we have an anemic response, right?

Admiral PANDOLFE. I think others are watching, and they are watching not just the response of the United States but the response of NATO, the response of the European Union, the response of the United Nations, and the entire system of international states, as is threatened by the actions of, in this case, Russia. And they are looking to see that the cost that we are threatening to— that we have imposed thus far and we are threatening to impose further should this aggression continue.

Mr. THORNBERRY. Well, I guess that leads me to wonder whether adding a few sentences to the QDR is enough of a reassessment. If it really is a paradigm shift, if it is that big a change, isn't it more logical that we need to make a bigger reassessment of our own capabilities, how much we spend, what our own approach to these security issues are?

Again, I think of it, especially from your view, not only what happens in Ukraine, but what happens in North Korea and Iran and the South China Sea and all these other places around the world.

Admiral PANDOLFE. Sir, as I mentioned in my first answer, the process of assessing risk, of allocating forces, and investing in relationships is an ongoing process. It never stops. It is shaped in each and every day by the actions in the world around us. And, clearly, the actions of Russia of late will impact our assessments as we move forward in those assessments.

Mr. THORNBERRY. Well, my last question is, do you think our process of reassessment is keeping up with the pace of events around the world?

Admiral PANDOLFE. I do. I think that we have a concerted and disciplined effort to try to measure risk. And we work very hard at it with the intelligence communities, with our colleagues, the State Department, the Office of Secretary of Defense.

And I think, as I mentioned a moment ago, it is a continuous process. We adjust as we go. But I think, fundamentally, the strategy as prescribed in the QDR is correct and that they have done a very nice job of looking around the world at the contending interests and values.

Mr. THORNBERRY. Okay.

I yield back.

The CHAIRMAN. Thank you.

Mr. Langevin.

Mr. LANGEVIN. Thank you, Mr. Chairman.

Mr. Secretary, Admiral, thank you very much for your testimony today and your service to our Nation.

I would like to start by going back to the chairman's question about Russian ability to project global power. And what is the current status of their aircraft carriers and their battle groups?

Admiral PANDOLFE. I would like to start by saying, in the closed session in an hour or so, there will be an intelligence official whose specialty is this kind of question.

My understanding, having operated in 6th Fleet up until about 6 months ago, is that the *Kuznetsov*, which is their last remaining carrier, is operational. It has a limited air wing of a few airplanes, if I remember correctly, something less than a dozen, and that it has periodically deployed to the Mediterranean and then come back to its northern Russian bases.

Mr. LANGEVIN. Very good. Thank you, Admiral.

Let me turn to something else. In January, Director Clapper stated that, and I quote, ''Following the measured improvements to Russian military capabilities in the past year, it is setting its sights on the long-term challenges of professionalization and rearmament. The military in the past year has taken an increasingly prominent role in out-of-the-area operations, most notably in the eastern Mediterranean but also in Latin America, the Arctic, and other regions, a trend that will probably continue,'' end quote.

He also stated, again I quote, ''Moscow is negotiating a series of agreements that would give it access to military infrastructure across the globe,'' end quote.

Could you provide any additional details about Russia's ambitions in these out-of-the-area operations and infrastructure access initiatives, and particularly whether and how those have changed after Russian occupation of the Crimea? And, again, further, what should be the United States' response?

Secretary CHOLLET. Well, sir, I can start. And as the Admiral said, I know in the closed part of this hearing today, our intelligence colleagues can provide a little bit more in terms of what Director Clapper was talking about.

Again, as the Admiral said in his opening statement, the Russians have embarked on a military modernization effort. It is something we have watched very closely. It is something that they started after the 2008 Georgia war and the shortcomings that they perceived in their military at that time.

I think we have seen some of the effect of that modernization, clearly, in Ukraine, particularly the special forces at work. And Russia has been, as you noted and as Director Clapper was quoted as saying, has been working to broaden out as much as it can, but still within a region. And I think its power projection is not global right now, but whether it is in the Arctic or whether it is in the Med, they are clearly trying to expand out.

That said, they are limited in what they can do. Despite their modernization efforts, they have tremendous challenges in their military in terms of the professionalization of the military and in terms of the demographics in their country, as well.

So, as I said, it is something we watch closely and we don't take lightly and we are focused on.

Admiral PANDOLFE. Yes, sir, I would agree with that.

From the reports I have read on their efforts toward professionalization and rearmament are that they have had some success, but it has been also mixed success in terms of the larger force. The force has gotten smaller; it has been streamlined. But as I understand it, the readiness is uneven, and the degree to which they have professionalized their military is incomplete. Nonetheless, they continue to work toward those goals. And they are long-term goals, as I understand it, for the Russian military.

In terms of out of area of operations, my observation is that they are relatively limited. They have operated heavily in the eastern Mediterranean in support of the Syrian Government, but, beyond that, I think that I would describe them as periodic and limited in scope.

Mr. LANGEVIN. Thank you, Admiral.

Turning to NATO, how have interactions within NATO changed since Russia's invasion of the Crimea? And with the show of aggression by the Russians, do you feel that it is more likely that more NATO member countries are going to begin to meet their treaty obligations for defense expenditures?

Secretary CHOLLET. Sir, the NATO consultations have been very intense. I don't know that—I wouldn't characterize it as a change. I would describe it more as an intensification of NATO meetings and engagements, in addition to, as I mentioned, more exercises. So I think that this has shown, this whole crisis has shown, the value of the strong transatlantic alliance and the investment we have made over many, many decades into NATO.

I hope—and we have a NATO summit coming up in Wales this September—I hope that this crisis is a proof point and will provide an impetus for those members who are not spending the kind of resources we would like to see on defense to spend more. But this has been an ongoing challenge we have faced for many years, in terms of getting more European governments to step up.

The CHAIRMAN. Thank you.

Mr. Jones.

Mr. JONES. Mr. Chairman, thank you very much.

And, Mr. Secretary, I am like most Members here in this committee; I have listened to testimony for the last 3 months from the service chiefs about all the problems facing our military, and this is going to bring me to my question in just one moment.

Mr. Putin obviously has been listening to the testimony by our service chiefs, as well. And even Secretary of Defense Hagel, who I have great respect for, has made comments that we are going to have to change the way that we organize our military and their functions and their responsibilities.

My concern—and I hear this back in my district, which is eastern North Carolina, the home of Camp Lejeune Marine Base and a couple of other bases—is that here we go again. The Nation—we are what is called a debtor nation. We have to borrow money, primarily from China, to fund our debt. And under George Bush, we raised the debt ceiling seven times in the 8 years that he was President of the United States. Under President Obama, we have raised the debt ceiling five times—seven times in 5 years.

This is the point I am trying to make. I hope in your discussions with primarily the Germans and the French and the Brits, I don't think that they have been as concerned or as engaged publicly— and maybe you can reassure me that I am wrong—in the fact that this primarily is their fight.

Now, I understand that we have these treaties, and I understand the role of NATO. And I do support NATO, by the way. But here we go again in trying to take the lead, so to speak, on this problem in Europe. And I think that, quite frankly, sometimes, instead of being the leader, we should be supporting these other nations, let them take the lead, let them be the ones that say to Putin, if you go any further, you are going to see the German troops or the French troops or the Brits.

Can you respond and give us any inside feelings, if not policy, but inside feelings, that they understand that this is their responsibility more than it is America's responsibility? And we want to be a team player, but we don't want to be captain of the team.

Secretary CHOLLET. Sir, great question.

First, I would like to say, I believe U.S. leadership remains indispensable. NATO is a collective security alliance; there are 28 partners. But we are the most consequential and important partner of that alliance.

But, second, I would say the Europeans clearly have close interests in what is happening in Ukraine and Russia's behavior. It is just in their neighborhood, it is much closer.

And the Europeans have stepped up in this crisis. Chancellor Merkel, for example, of Germany has been on the phone constantly with Putin and other senior Russian officials to make the very same arguments we have been making about the unacceptability of their actions. The EU, like the United States, the EU has stepped up in terms of sanctions, sanctioning Russian officials and other close allies of Putin in Moscow.

That is absolutely critical, because the ties between Europe and Russia are much stronger than the ties between the United States and Russia. So for any sanction to be meaningful, in terms of trying to get the attention of Russian officials, Europe has to be absolutely involved.

That is why, when President Obama was in Europe several weeks ago, he had a G–7 meeting on the margins of the Nuclear Security Summit and also very important talks in Brussels and then later in Rome about this crisis.

So I think that you are absolutely right, Europe has to be a part of this. I wouldn't say it is more their concern than ours. I would say it is our collective concern.

And Europeans are stepping up. I can provide for you—I don't have it off the top of my head. I have listed for you several examples in which the United States is contributing capabilities in Poland or the Balts to help reassure those NATO partners. The Europeans are doing so, as well. And we can provide you with some specifics on what other countries are doing to help reassure those countries that are most concerned about Russia's behavior.

Mr. JONES. Mr. Chairman, before I close—I got 29 seconds—I hope that the Administration—we were surprised, as Members of Congress, when we took military action against Libya. And I hope that if the Russians cross any line that would be of great concern to our country, that the President and his representatives would come to Congress and enlighten us as to what they are concerned about.

So I ask you, sir, to make sure that that message is passed back to the Administration.

Thank you.

The CHAIRMAN. Thank you.

Ms. Gabbard.

Ms. GABBARD. Thank you very much, Mr. Chairman.

I appreciate the opportunity to hear your insights on this, especially understanding that what has gone on in Ukraine is clearly not just about Ukraine and that we strategically really need to look at this with what Putin's end state is and that it is something far broader.

Mr. Chollet, you mentioned the biggest consequence—or the biggest cost that we can affect for Russia is its economy. But given the fact that, really, over a long period of time, strategically, they have distributed their energy supplies and really gotten to a point where they have a lot of leverage, what kind of consequence, realistically, can we set in the short term that will be meaningful and get a strong message to Putin without having unintended negative consequences on us?

Secretary CHOLLET. Well, as you mentioned at the end, that balance between ensuring we can have a consequence, particularly in the economic realm, that would be meaningful to Russia but not blow back on the United States is tricky sometimes.

I think that the economic sanctions we have already announced are going to have an effect. I think, as the President has outlined, we could do more along those lines if Russia's behavior continues along the course it has been on.

Third, I would not underestimate the impact of Russia's diplomatic isolation. As we saw just several months ago with the Winter Olympics, Mr. Putin very much enjoys the international spotlight. And he was planning this summer to host the G–8 [Group of Eight] leaders in Sochi. That meeting will not happen. And Russia is finding itself more and more alone in the world. And that will have an effect, as well.

So I think that there are steps we can take, there are steps, as I mentioned in the previous question, that our European allies can take and have taken to ensure that Russia feels the pinch economically and the consequences for its behavior but also is isolated in the world.

Ms. GABBARD. With regard to the military capabilities that you discussed, Russia's developments and really looking towards a more mobile special-force type operation, what can be done for Ukraine and possibly other bordering countries?

Knowing that a tank-to-tank kind of direct, one-on-one type of conflict is not realistic in any circumstance, how can we assist Ukraine to better defend itself using some of these similar unconventional means?

Secretary CHOLLET. We have had a pretty modest defense relationship with Ukraine over the years. It is a little over $4 million per year in FMF [Foreign Military Financing] that we have provided them. So the baseline we are working from is  relatively small.

That said, as I mentioned earlier, we have had ongoing consultations with the Ukrainians, not just about the urgent crisis of today but their needs of tomorrow and how they are working to reform and modernize their own military. That starts mainly in the nonlethal space, and it is things like helping with logistics. IMET [International Military Education and Training] has been very important for them, the education and exchanges, as they have tried to professionalize their military.

So there are ways that we can help. And we are actively working through those ideas with them, understanding that we are starting from a pretty modest baseline of defense support for them.

Admiral PANDOLFE. I would like to concur with that. Defense consultations were held in Kiev last week, and they looked at, amongst other things, you know, strengthening their defense establishment and building a program of training and exercises to help provide the kind of skills that you are referring to.

Ms. GABBARD. Good. I look forward to hearing more about that and, also, really, what kind of timeline is being looked at, considering what is happening, kind of, the updates on a minute-to-minute basis in eastern Ukraine. MREs are great and necessary and helpful, I am sure, but I am sure there are also many other ways that we could be of assistance in helping them or empowering them to be able to defend themselves.

Thank you.

I yield back, Mr. Chairman.

The CHAIRMAN. Thank you.

Mr. Wilson.

Mr. WILSON. Thank you, Mr. Chairman.

And thank both of you for being here today.

I have visited Russia a number of times, and I have been encouraged by the advance of free enterprise, of what I saw to be a level of democracy, but it is sad to see this extraordinary culture reverting to one-man control.

The benefits of economic freedom for Russia and its citizens are being undermined by isolating itself from being a law-abiding nation which is not trustworthy at home or abroad, with uncontrolled corruption destroying jobs.

With that in mind—and, again, it is really disappointing, because I just had such high hopes. And, indeed, we have a significant Russian-American population in my community that is truly in distress that things are going so badly at home with corruption.

With that in mind, what are our NATO allies doing in Central and Eastern Europe and the Baltics, reacting to Russia's aggression toward Ukraine? What are we doing to assure our allies and partners that the United States and NATO remain committed to deter aggression and preserve territorial integrity, in particularly the Baltic republics? What are we doing?

For each of you.

Secretary CHOLLET. Sir, first, I would just, on your opening comment, just to comment on that, I agree with you that Russia is not the Soviet Union——

Mr. WILSON. No.

Secretary CHOLLET [continuing]. And Russia has made great strides as a country and as a people over the last 20 years since the end of the Cold War. And we can see the great potential of that society. And that is why the events of the last several months are so disappointing and so alarming.

On to the question specifically about reassuring our partners, our close NATO allies, Poland and the Baltics, are very concerned about what is happening in Ukraine. This is something that—this is a nightmare unfolding for them.

And they are asking for our help. And that is why we have taken the steps we have already taken, in terms of deploying some assets there for exercises and training, to both send a message but also, on the ground, help the capabilities of our partners. That is why

General Breedlove has been tasked by NATO to look at further measures that we, as an alliance, can take, not just the United States but the United States and our NATO partners can take, to further reassure our allies.

And we have also stayed in very close touch at very high levels. The Vice President was in Poland and the Baltics several weeks ago for important consultations. Secretary Hagel, Secretary Kerry, the Chairman, the Joint Chiefs have all been in touch with their counterparts in the respective NATO countries. Secretary Kerry was in Brussels last week for an important NATO session. Secretary Hagel will be going to NATO again in June for another important session.

So we are trying to have a constant, ongoing dialogue with them about hearing their concerns, hearing their needs, and trying to address those as fast as possible.

Admiral PANDOLFE. Yes, sir, I would like to just build on that.

So, in the most immediate sense, we have sent additional fighter aircraft to the Baltic States to reinforce those that were there previously. We have done the same with Poland. So there are additional aircraft flowing to both of those locations. There has been additional tanker support sent to provide greater coverage. There are NATO AWACS aircraft flying orbits over Romania and Poland to provide greater situational awareness and support for those nations, as well. So these are the concrete steps that have been taken thus far to reassure our NATO allies.

And, as mentioned, the Foreign Ministers, when they met last week in Europe, directed General Breedlove to now formulate the next set of proposals to build on those actions and to come back to the NAC on the 15th. And he is doing that.

Mr. WILSON. And, Admiral, are the borders of the Baltic republics and Poland well-defined and -defended?

Admiral PANDOLFE. My understanding is they are well-defined. I would rather defer discussions of defense preparedness for the closed session.

Mr. WILSON. And I just can't imagine how important that will be. But, Mr. Secretary, again, the American people need to know——

Secretary CHOLLET. Right.

Mr. WILSON [continuing]. That, with the drawdown of the American military in Europe, I am concerned that this is giving encouragement to Russia on its aggression.

I am equally concerned, the last month, not only have we had this but we have had missile testing by North Korea. We have had Iran continue their enrichment of nuclear weapons and announce, in a visit by the Foreign Minister in Tokyo, that it is an illusion that they would stop. And we have had missiles being sent to Hamas in Gaza to threaten Israel, all in the last month. And, plus, China has expanded its air defense zone to threaten our allies in the Pacific.

All of this, I think, is an indication of weakness. And we know: Peace through strength.

Thank you very much.

Admiral PANDOLFE. Sir, before I would conclude my last answer, I want to reiterate that we do have Article 5 defense guarantees, security guarantees, with the Baltic States. That is clearly understood. And we will stand by those.

Mr. WILSON. And Poland.

Admiral PANDOLFE. And Poland, yes, sir.

Mr. WILSON. Thank you.

The CHAIRMAN. Thank you.

Mr. Enyart.

Mr. ENYART. Thank you, Mr. Chairman.

Gentlemen, the Russian military is still largely conscript.

I am all the way over here on stage left, all the way to your right, the lonely person all the way over here.

The Russian military is largely still conscript-based. Have we seen any changes—although they have been trying to move towards a more professional military, an all-volunteer force, they have yet to do that.

Have we seen any increase in the size of the conscript call-ups? Or have there been any moves towards the mobilization of reserve forces?

Admiral PANDOLFE. The Soviet military was about 4.3 million people. The current Russian military is less than 1 million. My understanding is that there are some conscripts still in that force, but there are also a number of volunteers now.

So there is not as much—I am not even—I don't even believe it is a majority conscript force any longer. So they have changed the complexion of the force.

As mentioned earlier, their efforts towards professionalization of the force have had some success, yet, not total success, because they do still rely on conscripts as well.

To the best of my knowledge—and we could have this followed up in the next session—I don't know of any changes in their call-ups of late.

Mr. ENYART. It is my understanding that Russia had been somewhat cooperative in regard to negotiations with Iran.

How is that progressing? Do you see a deterioration in that relationship?

Secretary CHOLLET. We have not yet, sir. Russia has played a role in the P5+1 [Five permanent members of the U.N. Security Council plus Germany] process with Iran. Russia also, as you know, has been a part of the effort to get Syria's chemical weapons out of that country.

And, so far, we have not seen any appreciable impact on those efforts as a result of our deep differences over this Ukraine crisis.

Mr. ENYART. I just had, immediately prior to walking into this hearing, I had three Polish officers come visit me in my office. And they were veterans of Afghanistan, and several of them had served with soldiers that I used to command in the Illinois National Guard in Afghanistan.

And I am certainly glad to hear you saying that we will stand by our NATO commitments, and I would anticipate that we would stand by our NATO commitments, because I assured them that, just as they have stood by us in Iraq and in Afghanistan for the last dozen years, that we would stand by our NATO commitments.

As we draw out of Afghanistan, do you see that this will free up our hand, that is, give us greater logistics capacity, to otherwise respond in Central Europe or around the world, as need be?

Secretary CHOLLET. Sir, first on Poland, I just want to reiterate that Poland is a terrific partner of ours. We have very, very close defense relations.

Poland is one of the European countries that is stepping up and spending a significant amount of resources on its own defense and seeking to modernize its military, and that is an effort that we are helping them with.

I was with Secretary Hagel in Warsaw several months ago for a visit, and we are looking forward to hosting the Defense Ministry here in Washington soon. So we are in very close touch with our Polish partners.

In terms of how retrograde out of Afghanistan may help us, you know, that is something that we are sorting through in terms of having that material be freed up.

One of the discussions we have ongoing—it is not related to the Ukraine crisis, but it is related to the Afghanistan point—is many countries around the world, not just in Europe, talked to us about perhaps acquiring some of that equipment as excess defense articles, as they are seeking to modernize and replenish their militaries.

So that is something we are taking a close look at as part of this ongoing reassessment that the admiral discussed that we are constantly doing as a result of this crisis.

Mr. ENYART. Just one final comment, as I am almost out of time.

But when I was frequently in Central Europe during my previous occupation, I frequently told our NATO friends that, in my view, when we have peace in Central Europe, we have peace, relatively speaking, in the world. And so I think this clearly is a very critical situation that we have to deal with.

I yield back.

Mr. THORNBERRY [presiding]. Mr. Turner.

Mr. TURNER. Thank you, Mr. Chairman.

Admiral, General Breedlove, the Supreme Allied Commander for Europe, was in town about a week ago meeting with Members. Loretta Sanchez and I hosted a bipartisan briefing that he participated in. Carol Shea-Porter was with us.

And the commander publicly released to us that there were 80,000 troops that constituted—that had been mobilized by Russia on the border of Ukraine that constituted an invasion-ready force.

In classified setting, he went over how he gets to that number and what it was constituted of, which, of course, I won't go into today, but he described to us, disclosed to us, how that number was derived.

There are a number of other numbers that are being circulated. Ukraine says 80- to 100,000. The State Department began to say 40-. Now the Department of Defense is saying 40- seems to be a wild range of what those numbers are.

Quite frankly, I trust the Supreme Allied Commander General Breedlove to know what he is facing, and he has publicly said it is 80-.

But regardless of the wide swing of the number, Admiral, I would appreciate it if you would give us some description or understanding of the magnitude of that force. I think, quite frankly, that there has not been enough public discussion, and certainly it is something that we can discuss publicly. Google Earth can tell you a lot about what we are seeing.

What is the magnitude of that force's capabilities? Breedlove is describing it as an invasion-ready force. What do you see when you look at the type of equipment capabilities that are being amassed on the border of Ukraine?

Admiral PANDOLFE. Well, like you, I spoke with General Breedlove about this, and I will leave the numbers and how we get to different sets of numbers for the next session, where the intelligence experts can walk us through that.

But what General Breedlove made clear is it is a substantial force. It is a very large force. It is extraordinarily capable, in our estimation.

It is a combined armed force. So you have fixed-wing and rotor-wing aircraft. You have armored units. You have artillery. You have light infantry.

And we have seen, as part of results of the modernization of the Russian military, their ability to employ these different elements of military power in a synchronized and integrated manner.

So it is a threat which we are taking very seriously. General Breedlove, Secretary General of NATO, and others have been very clear about this, and we are watching it very closely.

Mr. TURNER. Thank you.

Secretary, the—there are a number of voices that say that we are not doing enough, Washington Post being one. This is an editorial from the Washington Post. It says, ''President Obama's foreign policy is based on fantasy.''

The walk-off line of the editorial is, ''As Mr. Putin ponders whether to advance further into Eastern Ukraine, say, he will measure the success of U.S. and allied actions, not their statements.''

This is not a partisan statement. This is the Washington Post. I ask that this editorial be entered into the record.

[The information referred to can be found in the Appendix on page 59.]

Mr. TURNER. Sending MREs is basically expanding our school lunch program. That is the equivalency. It certainly isn't strong actions. I am very concerned that we are not doing enough to actually assist the Ukrainians in giving military advice and assistance.

If Russia does go into Ukraine and the Ukraines decide and desire to defend themselves, certainly our advice and—both as to what they are facing and as to their military configuration would be important. Many people have called for that.

We definitely see a Russia that has changed course. We now have a standing use of—authorizing use of force to Putin by his parliament that includes areas of Estonia, Latvia, Lithuania, Poland, and Romania, because he said all Russians that are in non-Russian territory.

In looking at your background and working with the Dayton Peace Accords and Holbrooke and Talbott and being from Dayton, I have a high regard for your background and expertise.

Shouldn't we be doing more? And what else can we be doing besides just MREs?

Secretary CHOLLET. Sir, thanks for your question.

First, I think we are doing a lot to support Ukraine. What Ukraine really needs badly is help with its economy. That is why the IMF decision was very important. That is why——

Mr. TURNER. Sir, just a second.

With all due respect, their economy is going to be irrelevant if we wait a few more weeks. Right? Because they are just going to be——

Secretary CHOLLET. Well, they need urgent help. And I think that the assistance we can provide, the Europeans can provide—and we are grateful to the Congress for the assistance that you have decided on—is very important, number one.

Mr. TURNER. Don't you think military assistance is what they really need if they are going to be facing an invasion, advice, a description as to what is coming over the hill?

Secretary CHOLLET. So, as we discussed earlier, we had a team in Kiev last week for defense consultation talks, a joint civilian-military team to talk through both what they need for this urgent crisis and what they need for the future.

And they have prioritized. Nonlethal assistance first. And the MREs are very urgent for them. It is something that they need. They had troops in the field who needed it because they needed resupply. So that is meaningful to them that they are getting this.

And we are talking through with them further requests for support, and that is something we will be working through in the coming days.

Mr. THORNBERRY. The time of the gentleman is expired.

Mr. Scott.

Mr. SCOTT. Thank you, Mr. Chairman.

Many of the questions that—I have already been asked. I guess, again, I want to reiterate the point that, in our QDR, there was very little focus on Russia.

If there is a rewrite of the QDR, what focus do you expect in that document would be placed on Russia?

Secretary CHOLLET. Well, Congressman, we are not planning a rewrite of the QDR. That said, I think that it is—as we have acknowledged, if we were to rewrite it at this moment, there would be some—certainly some language changes because the world is dynamic and it is always changing and what has happened over the last several weeks since the QDR was put to press is very significant.

But, to repeat, I think the fundamental strategy outlined in the QDR and the budget that the Secretary and the chairman have outlined before you is one that will fulfill our interests and help us respond to this crisis.

Mr. SCOTT. Let me ask, then. It seems that a lot of the focus—and you keep going back to the economy and our friends over there in needing economic support. There is also a way to hurt the Russians right now.

I mean, their economy depends on the price of a barrel of oil in many cases. And, you know, you have—the President refuses to sign the Keystone Pipeline bill that, quite honestly, would drop the price of a barrel of oil and potentially hurt Putin.

Has that played into these discussions in any way, shape, or form? I mean, is—the ability to drop the price of a barrel of oil and what that would do to the Russians?

Secretary CHOLLET. Not at the Pentagon. That conversation has not come up, although the discussion of how we might further impact the Russian economy in terms of any response to what Russia may do here on out is something that has come under discussion.

And the President has publicly announced that he is—has the authority to have sectorial sanctions, which could include the Russian energy industry.

But I want to be clear that those are not necessarily cost-free exercises in terms of our own interest. So we want to be very careful with how we execute on something like that, but Russia's behavior could lead us to that.

Mr. SCOTT. But sending F–16s and MREs—really, dropping the price of a barrel of oil would do more to—in response to the Russian's actions than sending F–16s and MREs, wouldn't it?

Secretary CHOLLET. Well, the F–16s and MREs are more about reassuring our partners and showing them, in deed as well as word, that we have got their back, that we are committed to Article 5 and we are committed to working with them.

Clearly, Russia has been riding its energy industry for many years now. So anything we might be able to do to impact its energy sector would have an impact.

Mr. SCOTT. Well, what do you think—you know, what do you think Putin thinks belongs to him? I mean, is he trying to put the whole motherland back together?

Secretary CHOLLET. Again, I always hesitate to try to get into Putin's head. He has said publicly that the collapse of the Soviet Union was a great historical tragedy.

That is obviously something I think certainly this Administration, all of the American people, most of the world, disagree with.

And Russia's actions seem to indicate a view that having client states around its periphery is in its interest. We have a very different view.

We do not believe that decisions can be made about those countries without those countries involved. The Ukrainian people should have a choice for their own destiny.

We don't deny that Russia has legitimate interests and a long history with Ukraine. It is the cradle of Russian civilization, after all.

Mr. SCOTT. Okay. But——

Secretary CHOLLET. But there is a right way and a wrong way to go about addressing this.

Mr. SCOTT [continuing]. Isn't the key question whether or not Putin stops or he has to be stopped?

Secretary CHOLLET. We believe that Russia's behavior at this point, its actions in Crimea, absolutely unacceptable, and there have been consequences.

Mr. SCOTT. Do you think it stops——

Secretary CHOLLET. Further actions, so far, we have been very concerned about his build-up of troops on the border. So far, those have not moved, but we are watching that very closely and making it clear that, if his actions continue, that there will be consequences.

Mr. SCOTT. Are they moving supply lines in, though?

I mean, obviously, when you put your troops forward, you have got to put supply lines in for fuel and for food and for other things.

Are they pushing supply lines forward so that they can keep those troops that are at the front supplied?

Secretary CHOLLET. Sir, if I could, I would like to bring that to the closed part of the session to get a greater description of what is going on on the eastern border.

Mr. SCOTT. Thank you, Mr. Chairman.

Mr. THORNBERRY. Thank you.

Mr. Barber.

Mr. BARBER. Thank you, Mr. Chairman.

And thanks to our witnesses for being here today.

I want to, Admiral, if I could with you, delve into the whole issue of intelligence gathering.

The recent developments with the Russian military in the Ukrainian crisis I think bring up some very serious questions about how we get information that allows us to take appropriate action and be out in front of things.

So I would like to ask for your perspective, Admiral, on the importance of intelligence gathering and how it helps develop our strategy when a crisis such as the annexation of Crimea occurs.

As you may know, I represent Fort Huachuca in southern Arizona. It is home to Army Intelligence Center of Excellence, which is an important aspect in our human intelligence capabilities. And many of the soldiers that come through Fort Huachuca play a critical role in DOD's [Department of Defense's] intelligence gathering.

However, it seems to me that much of the current focus on intelligence, Admiral, revolves around technical capabilities, such as surveillance and reconnaissance platforms and cyber capabilities.

Human intelligence, however, has long been a staple of our collection capabilities, accessing populations and information that technical approaches cannot reach.

So given the focus on tactical human intelligence, or HUMINT, for the past 13 years in Afghanistan and Iraq, are the current HUMINT assets in the European Command's area of responsibility sufficiently prepared or resourced for an Eastern European mission set?

And can you tell me, Admiral, how critical a role do these assets have in the particular situation we are here to talk about today between Ukraine and Russia as it continues to develop? Admiral.

Admiral PANDOLFE. Well, it is very difficult to talk about the specifics of intelligence in an open hearing. I would be happy, again, to take this further in the closed hearing.

Writ large, however, clearly intelligence at all levels—strategic, tactical—of all types—technical, human—is very, very important and it has to be worked into a holistic view of not only what is happening, but what will happen next. And that is an art as well as a science. And we work at it very hard.

So I will leave it at that, but I think we can pick this theme up again later and give you more details of—that answer your specific questions.

Mr. BARBER. Yeah. I really would like to have that further briefing. I understand that some of this cannot be discussed in an open meeting—or an open hearing.

But, you know, there have been a lot of criticisms. Did we know what was going on? Did we know that troops were amassing? What did we try to do? Were we positioning ourselves? And if we could get to that in another setting, that would be very helpful.

And I guess the final question, Admiral, is: Do you think the DOD budget cuts, as a main concern of all of us, the services' personnel reductions, our Nation's strategic pivot to the Asia-Pacific region, and the drawdown of forces in Afghanistan—could they, do you believe, have a negative effect on our ability and our missions for HUMINT collections capabilities for the Eastern European area or perhaps could they enhance it?

Admiral PANDOLFE. That is a very specific question regarding the impact of a wide set of efficiencies on a specific area. I don't know of how these cuts would necessarily impact that particular area in a negative way.

I can research that for you, however, and come back—take that for the record and come back with a more focused answer.

[The information referred to is classified and retained in the committee files.]

Mr. BARBER. If you could, that would be helpful.

I am concerned, as I think many Members are, that it doesn't—a month doesn't go by that we don't have another front, it seems, opening up.

You know, we have been dealing with Afghanistan, Iraq, Africa, the Middle East, of course. And now we are dealing with Russia and the Russian Federation, apparently, Putin's ambition to rebuild the Soviet Empire.

And now our attention has to—must turn to the European theater and the European region and how we staff it on many levels not only in terms of troops on the ground and air assets and Navy assets, but how we inform ourselves about what next move this empire builder might have.

So it would be helpful if we could get a sense of where you are headed, given what has happened in Crimea, which I think most people 6 months ago would not have imagined would have been going on.

So how are we positioning ourselves to deal with his future ambitions would be helpful to know.

Admiral PANDOLFE. Yes, sir. I will get back to you on that.

Mr. BARBER. Thank you, Mr. Chairman.

I yield back.

The CHAIRMAN [presiding]. Mr. Lamborn.

Mr. LAMBORN. Thank you, Mr. Chairman.

Secretary Chollet, the Russians are flagrantly in violation of the Budapest Memorandum concerning Ukraine. Russia is a serious, strongest supporter and a consistent ally of Iran.

President Obama immediately after his election cancelled the third site missile defense plan with Poland and the Czech Republic, which pleased Putin.

How could President Obama's and Secretary Hillary Clinton's highly touted Russian reset have failed so spectacularly? What did you do wrong?

Secretary CHOLLET. Sir, I think even though we are very disappointed with where we are with Russia today, we saw some tangible impact of our policies in the first several years of this Administration under a different Russian leadership with President Medvedev, but the work with them on Iran, for example, was something that was very important. We also codified a new arms reduction agreement on nuclear forces, which was very significant.

And even since then, we have seen Russian cooperation in other areas, for example, on Syria in the chemical weapons destruction process, which continues. Even despite the turbulence of this crisis and the U.S.-Russian relationship, we have been able to maintain our cooperation on that very, very important issue.

So while, I think, even the President and everyone involved in the U.S.-Russian relationship over the last several years are not happy with where we are today, we do believe that we had some successes early on in this Administration.

Mr. LAMBORN. Well, I would really question a lot of that assessment.

And let's talk about the New START Treaty. According to recent press reports and open sources, the Russian Federation is in violation of the Intermediate-Range Nuclear Forces Treaty, or INF, which this Administration has known about for some time, but has chosen to remain quiet about.

Why is the Administration covering up Russian INF treaty violations? Is it an attempt to protect the deeply flawed New START Treaty?

Secretary CHOLLET. Sir, we have—we take our treaty obligations very seriously and we expect all of our—those who enter into a treaty to take their obligations very seriously. So the INF issue is something we have been studying very closely.

I know that colleagues of ours have been talking to the Congress throughout this process, and I know that the State Department, which is the lead in our interagency for this effort, will be issuing a report on this matter soon.

And perhaps some of the specifics you have referred to we can get into in the closed session later today.

Mr. LAMBORN. Well, I hope that what you did wrong wasn't to think that authoritarian regimes respond to reason rather than to strength. I think they respond to strength better than to reason.

Thank you, Mr. Chairman. I yield back.

The CHAIRMAN. Thank you.

Ms. Duckworth.

Ms. DUCKWORTH. Thank you, Mr. Chairman.

I thank you so much for being here, gentlemen.

I am a little concerned about our allies' contributions in NATO itself. NATO clearly has a significant role to play in this crisis. But I am concerned about its ability to leverage its limited capabilities that it has.

In 2013, I believe, only three European nations—Estonia, Greece, and the United Kingdom—contributed the required 2 percent or more of their GDP [gross domestic product].

Another three nations—France, Turkey, and Poland—each gave 1.9 and 1.8 percent, respectively. We contribute approximately 70 percent of the NATO budget.

Could you explain for us the current state of our NATO allies' military and the current role they are playing in the Ukrainian crisis and whether they can respond decisively, given these levels of commitment?

Secretary CHOLLET. Ma'am, you have highlighted a great concern of ours and something we have been working on for many years, as you know, trying to work with our European partners to spend at least 2 percent of their GDP on defense and to try to spend that—spend those resources wisely.

As I mentioned in a previous question—and some specifics we can follow up with you on after this—it is not only the United States that have been contributing some capability to theater in the past several weeks in response to the Ukraine crisis as a way to reassure our partners. Other countries—the Brits, the Germans, the French, the Poles themselves—have as well. And we can give you some of the specifics on that as part of followup.

But it doesn't—it doesn't obviate the basic point that you made, which is there is a capabilities gap that is widening. It is something that many Secretaries of Defense, going back at least to Secretary Gates, have talked about. And it is one of the big pieces of business we are going to try to address this summer—or this fall, in September, at the Wales NATO Summit, how, moving forward, we can ensure that the NATO alliance collectively, each member in its own way, can be stepping up meaningfully to deal with security threats as they come our way.

Ms. DUCKWORTH. One of the components of this is the relationship through the State Partnership Programs, something that has been incredibly important and something that EUCOM commander, AFRICOM [U.S. Africa Command] commander, Special Forces, have all said has been a vital part of their operations. Especially in the case of Poland, the State of Illinois has been in the State Partnership Program with Poland for almost 25 years now. It is one of the first in the Nation to do that.

That is a very special relationship. That is, you know, I watched my Polish counterparts grow up as I grew up in the military together. And I was—I would think that, as nations like Poland are starting to step up to take the lead among NATO allies with what is happening in the Ukraine and in that region of the world, that that State Partnership Program would be even more important as we move forward.

Can you speak a little bit to the program and how you see it changing or growing or its role in this crisis.

Secretary CHOLLET. The State Partnership Programs we have with Poland—and I am very familiar with Illinois' great cooperation with Poland over many years—but throughout Central and Eastern Europe have paid great dividends over the years, and these are extremely important relationships to our partner countries.

Every single Defense Minister that comes into the Pentagon that Secretary Hagel sees will mention the importance of the State Partnership Program that they have, and often, as you know, these Defense Ministers, when they visit Washington, will also visit the State where they have a partnership.

And it is not just something that—where they have helped with training and exercises, but they have deployed in the field together in places like Afghanistan.

So I think it was with a great vision and foresight several decades ago that the State Partnership Program was established. It is something that we deeply believe in, and work to augment and support in any way we can.

Ms. DUCKWORTH. Thank you.

What type of missions are our allies, the NATO allies, performing right now? And are they adequately equipped to perform these missions effectively in this region as part of NATO and how are our allies forces——

Secretary CHOLLET. And this is in terms of the Ukraine crisis?

Ms. DUCKWORTH. Yes.

Secretary CHOLLET. Well, as I said, we can get you some specifics on exactly what every country is contributing in their own way. And I guess I will stress in their own way. They are capable with what they are contributing. I think, overall, we would like to see more capability within the alliance across the board.

But it is not just the United States that has been stepping up in the last several months. Other of our closest partners, the Brits and the Germans in particular, have been working in their own way, but also along the similar lines of us. It is about exercises. It is about training and working with the Balts and the Poles in particular to try to reassure them.

Ms. DUCKWORTH. Thank you.

I yield back, Mr. Chairman.

The CHAIRMAN. Thank you.

Mr. Franks.

Mr. FRANKS. Well, thank you, Mr. Chairman.

Thank you all for being here.

Admiral Pandolfe, thank you for your 35 years, I think now, of service to the cause of freedom.

Supreme Allied Commander General Breedlove recently stated in regard to the Russian violation of Intermediate Range and Nuclear Forces Treaty by testing a ground-launched cruise missile—and he said, ''This is a militarily significant development. Weapon capability that violates the INF that is introduced into the greater European landmass is absolutely a tool that will have to be dealt with. It can't go unanswered.''

The recently released QDR mentions cooperation with Russia 10 times to include further reductions in our nuclear deterrent. While it obviously was drafted before the events unfolded in Ukraine, it was drafted with full knowledge of the Russian INF treaty violations.

And, further, the Administration has succumbed to Russian objections that halted the missile defense field planned for Poland and a radar site in the Czech Republic.

And given all of the present events, I mean, I am wondering what plans or capability this Administration has, Mr. Chollet, to counter this Russian—I mean, other than perhaps threatening to do to the Russian economy what they have done to ours. I mean, that is a little drastic.

But what, in terms of military capability, do we have arrayed there that would be any deterrent to the Russian efforts there, again, given these comments I have just made?

Secretary CHOLLET. Well, Congressman, we have significant military capability in the European theater, but, also, capability elsewhere that could be surged to the European theater in case we were in a situation where we were implementing our Article 5 commitment to the NATO alliance, the collective defense commitment that we take as a member of NATO.

So—and we have been very clear with the Russians that we take Article 5 seriously, that we are unwavering in our support for our European partners.

And we have tried to demonstrate that unwavering support through several of our actions, including the deployment of some aircraft to the Baltics and Poland in particular, which is very significant for those countries and has been warmly welcomed and has gotten a lot of attention.

And we are considering further steps we may take to reassure those partners and other Central and Eastern European partners, and that is an effort that General Breedlove has undertaken. And we expect in the next week or so he will have some more concrete ideas that he can share with us.

Mr. FRANKS. Well, I won't count on that except to say that it appears that Mr. Putin hasn't gotten the memo.

Prior to the invasion of Crimea, Russian forces were obviously very prepared. They were trained. They were ready for the mission. And, meanwhile, NATO forces were not.

Has this Administration arrayed forces that would be the kind of deterrent to Russia in that region that—sort of a follow-on to the question.

But, more importantly, how has the budgetary limitations that may be affecting our force posture in the EUCOM—how have you proposed to try to address that?

Secretary CHOLLET. And, sir, I would say it wasn't as though we were unprepared. Ukraine, of course, is not a member of NATO. But the NATO alliance——

Mr. FRANKS. But we have that little Budapest agreement with them. I mean, you know, it is not like—I am sort of astonished that we have stepped back from that. I mean, of course, Russia has done so in an even more dramatic fashion.

Secretary CHOLLET. Yeah. And it wasn't an Article 5 agreement where there is a commitment——

Mr. FRANKS. So it really wasn't that big a deal. Right?

Secretary CHOLLET. Oh, no. It was a very big deal. And the fact that Russia has violated every letter of that agreement is a huge concern for us.

But we have been working very closely with our NATO partners to ensure that they have the capability that they need and that, if necessary, we augment that capability with our own to make clear that the Article 5 commitment holds.

The budget environment has clearly had an impact around the world on the U.S. military. That is no secret. And that is why we have sought to try to do some innovative things, for example, these rotational deployments that we launched several years ago in Poland where F–16s and C–130s will rotate through Poland, will exercise with our Polish partners, will train with them, and then rotate out.

It is not a permanent presence, but it is something that, particularly in this budgetary environment, pays great dividends moving forward.

So we have augmented that as a result of this most recent crisis, and we are exploring ways to further develop exercises along those lines.

Mr. FRANKS. Admiral Pandolfe, would you give us just your best insight as to what this committee and the country's response should be related to the Ukraine crisis.

Admiral PANDOLFE. I think the courses of action laid out by Mr. Chollet make great sense. I mean, clearly, we want to continue to provide assistance to Ukraine, and we are doing that primarily by economic avenues.

But we are also considering—"we" being the Administration—other requests that they have. We are reinforcing our NATO allies to assure them of their security, and we are making clear to the Russians that their actions are going to cost them and their people and their future significantly.

I mean, their economy is now intertwined in the global economy. It is not the Soviet Union. Their stock market is down significantly. They can't get investment into their energy fields, which is how they generate their income. They can't get people to buy their debt. I mean, the future of Russia is going to suffer because of the actions of this government.

We have made that clear and we have made clear that there is more to come—much more to come of a more serious nature should they continue this aggressive action contrary to their promises and to international law.

Mr. FRANKS. I yield back.

Mr. NUGENT [presiding]. The gentleman's time is expired.

Mr. Smith is recognized.

Mr. SMITH. Thank you, Mr. Chairman.

I just want to explore a little bit this option—or this notion that, you know, there must be something more that we could do that could cause Putin to change his mind, because I think we all share that frustration.

He is making decisions that, as you have stated, do not appear to be in the best interest of his own country, certainly threatens stability. We wish we could just make him stop.

So I have a little bit of a preamble here, but then I have a question about, you know, what more could we be doing. Because I do want to challenge a little bit this notion that somehow, you know, aggression always responds better to aggression than appeasement.

I think that is what has led to many, many wars, is the notion that we always have to ramp it up in order to show the other side that we are serious and then, of course, the other side is thinking, "Well, we have to ramp it up, too, in order to show we are serious" and pretty soon you are at war.

I mean, you can look at World War I and that is exactly what happened. Nobody wanted to appease anybody and, at the end of the day, they said, "Well, we have made this commitment. So we just got to do it" and millions of people died and there was a horrific impact on Europe.

And then, of course, after World War I, you know, we could not possibly have been more aggressive with Germany after they were defeated. You know, we sort of pounded them economically and in all manner of different ways and we all saw how that turned out.

So this notion that, if we are somehow just tough enough with an irrational adversary, that will lead to good things, is one that I always want to make sure does not stand unchallenged because it can lead to some very, very bad results.

Now, further, in dealing with Russia specifically, many of the Russia experts that I talked to back in the 1990s at the University of Washington and elsewhere felt that our decision to expand NATO was one of the things that made Russia feel insecure and sort of pushed them towards Putin and made Putin's argument easy. "See, the West is coming for us."

Now moving into Eastern Europe and sort of caused that backlash of the strength we showed in expanding NATO and then, to some degree, arming some of the former Soviet satellite states, you know, led to the reaction of Putin and his leadership.

Now, I am not suggesting that there is any sort of easy way to do that. I just want to counter the notion that somehow, if you just show strength, this all goes away. There is very, very little historical precedent for that being true.

So with that as sort of a preamble, what would we do right now?

You know, there is frustration on the panel and everyone else. "We need to do more. If we just did more, if we showed we were serious, then Putin would turn back around."

I do always like to remind everybody that, you know, the U.S. military was never stronger than it was in 2008. We—you know, $700 billion a year we were spending. I think, at that point, we were spending more money on our defense than the entire rest of the world combined.

We had just invaded two countries and deposed their leadership, and Putin went in and basically annexed two parts of Georgia in the midst of that. So, obviously, strength alone is not the answer in there. It comes with considerable risk.

So as you are looking at the options here, you know, and people are saying, "Do more," what would "do more" look like?

And I have heard your answer, and I tend to agree with it, that, basically, we are showing the Russian people that Putin's actions are hurting them, that their economy is going down when it wasn't that high to begin with and, eventually, that begins to have an impact.

But if we were to sort of, you know, step back for a moment and say, "Let's accept this notion that somehow, if we just appeared to be strong enough, Putin would for some reason abandon all of his perceived interests," what would that look like? What is it that we would do to show that we were ''being stronger'' to change his calculus?

Secretary CHOLLET. Well, Congressman, I very much appreciate your comment and agree with almost everything you have said.

In terms of what we could do more, it is along the lines of operation that we have outlined here for you this morning. General Breedlove is currently looking at ways we can do more to reassure our NATO partners and to explore ways that, in the near term, but over in the medium and long term, we can strengthen the ties that we have through NATO, improve their military capabilities, the interoperability that the alliance has developed over these now—this decade-plus of war together in Afghanistan.

So that is more, and that is something we may do, regardless of whatever Putin's next move is.

Mr. SMITH. I agree with you.

But specifically to the Ukraine, I mean, what you just described are sort of the options that are considered not enough.

But where the Ukraine is concerned, I mean, have you seriously considered, you know, arming the Ukraine specifically and say, ''Hey, Russia is coming. We are going to start arming you to the teeth and fight a proxy war with them''?

Secretary CHOLLET. So our overall approach throughout this entire crisis has been we seek to deescalate tensions and that, as the President has been very clear about, there is not a military solution to the Ukrainian crisis.

That said, we have been in very close touch with our Ukrainian counterparts throughout the crisis and most recently last week with an expert team in Kiev, talking with them about the urgent needs they have, but, also, their medium- to long-term plan for their own military modernization and reform, which has a ways to go. Let's be honest.

Mr. SMITH. Right. That is an understatement.

Secretary CHOLLET. So there is certainly more we can do. And what we are doing is trying to be thoughtful and work through with them on what the next steps may be.

Now, whether or not that has any effect on Mr. Putin's mindset is anyone's guess, but it also just may be the right thing to do, anyway.

Mr. SMITH. Yeah. No. I think it is the right thing to do, anyway.

But Mr. Putin's mindset, I can't see it having an impact. His mindset is based on—you know, I think has been correctly described that, basically, he wants to build a—he wants to return Russia to its glory, basically.

His mistake is in perceiving how to do that. The devastating and economically annexing small parts of the former Soviet Union are not going to lead to that result. And I think what we have to do is convince him of that.

Thank you.

I yield back.

Mr. NUGENT. Mr. Coffman is recognized for 5 minutes.

Mr. COFFMAN. Thank you, Mr. Chairman.

And thank you so much, both of you, for your dedicated service to our country.

I was in the United States Army's 1st Armored Division in the early 1970s, along to fill the gap in then West—the West German-Czechoslovakian border, and it was really a great demonstration of peace through strength in terms of, I think, what was a very effective containment policy, containment doctrine, in terms of the Soviet Union and its Warsaw Pact allies.

And it seems that we were lulled in—and justifiably so—in the aftermath of the fall of the Soviet Union that NATO had to—NATO needed a new mission. NATO had to be repurposed. And so we looked at deploying NATO to places like Afghanistan.

It seems like now we need to take NATO back to its original purpose of being a buffer to Russian expansion in the region.

And so, first of all, I commend you in terms of your comment by saying that, you know, it is rotational forces. It is joint military exercises as opposed to the reestablishment of a large U.S. military permanent presence that we had in Western Europe when I was there.

I think we can more effectively demonstrate our support for our NATO allies, but I am concerned—and this was raised earlier in testimony—about the commitment of our allies—our NATO allies.

And we, in terms of exercising U.S. leadership, need to convince our allies that they need to step up to the plate in terms of defense spending, that this cannot be on—the burden, on the backs, of the U.S. military and U.S. taxpayers.

And so what can we do to get our NATO allies to be the necessary force multiplier in order to be that buffer to Russian expansion by at least going to 2 percent of gross domestic—of defense—GDP spending, 2 percent as a minimum?

Secretary CHOLLET. Sir, first, thank you for your service in Europe and elsewhere.

And you have, you know, put your finger on what is the key issue, and it is something that we have been working for many years, but, also, have been frustrated by for many years, which is the defense spending and capabilities of some of our NATO partners.

And that Article 5 commitment has always remained the cornerstone of the NATO alliance. Even over the last two decades, there was—NATO has gone out of area, whether first in the Balkans, counter-piracy mission, but, of course, most notably in Afghanistan.

So we work very closely with our partners to try to encourage them and, also, help them make the case to their own publics about spending greater resources on defense.

We at the Defense Department try to work with our defense colleagues around NATO countries to help them make smart decisions about what systems to buy and how we might be able to help them think through that.

I also think this is an area where the Congress and all of you on the committee and your counterparts in the House and over on the Senate side have a very important role to play as well.

Because, as you know, these are political decisions in these NATO democracies, political decisions about how much money and resources to spend. And the European economies have been suffering as much or, in many cases, way more than the United States economy.

And so working with your counterparts to help make the case for why it is important for all 28 NATO allies, not just the United States and a handful of others, to maintain that 2 percent threshold and a strong robust spending on defense.

But there is no silver bullet here. This is not something that we are going to be able to solve with one speech or one effort.

It is something that we are constantly working on, whether it is bilaterally or whether it is the NATO summit this September in Wales in which capabilities will be a big theme of the summit in Wales.

And I think the Ukraine crisis, if anything else—if there is a silver lining to anything that has happened here, it has helped remind everyone of the importance of the Transatlantic Partnership and NATO specifically, but also been a reminder to all of us and our European partners in particular about the importance of having a strong defense and spending the necessary resources that have that.

Mr. COFFMAN. I am running out of time here, but I want to make a statement here that I had met with the ambassador from Hungary to the United States just prior to the Russian incursion into Crimea.

And what he informed me that the most important thing that the United States could do would be to export LNG, or liquefied national gas, to break the Russian hold on Europe in terms of its dependence on energy resources.

With that, Mr. Chairman, I yield back.

Mr. NUGENT. Dr. Wenstrup is recognized for 5 minutes.

Dr. WENSTRUP. Thank you, Mr. Chairman.

Do you have concerns that Russia could restrict the parts that are needed for the helicopters that have been sold to the Afghan National Security Forces?

Secretary CHOLLET. Sir, we do.

Dr. WENSTRUP. And so how are we approaching that, if we are at all, to try to assure that the Afghan forces will be adequately taken care of?

Secretary CHOLLET. Sir, you are touching on an issue that we thought a lot about and I know we talked with you and this committee about, and that is the Russian supply of the Mi-17 helicopters, which is a critical capability for the Afghan National Security Forces [ANSF] as they are seeking to develop.

And that is why we have been very mindful and careful when we have gone about contemplating certain sanctions to ensure that our other interests, a strong ANSF in Afghanistan, are being served.

So we have an existing contract with a Russian entity that is supplying those Mi-17 helicopters. We are seeking to complete that contract and expedite it as much as possible and, if necessary, look for ways to mitigate any sort of disruption in the supply.

Dr. WENSTRUP. What is our role in that supply line? I mean, will they—the maintenance of these aircraft, is that coming directly from Russia? Is it coming through us? What is our role in that negotiation?

Secretary CHOLLET. Sir—and I want to get back to you more specifically, but my understanding is our role is in support of the

ANSF, but it is the Russians who actually have the knowledge of how to operate these aircraft and maintain them.

Dr. WENSTRUP. Well, I would think certainly within our military we have people that are familiar with those aircraft.

So my question is: Are we part of that supply line? Is it coming through U.S. means and then being delivered to the Afghans or are they getting it directly?

Secretary CHOLLET. Yeah. I don't—sir, I want to get back to you specifically.

Dr. WENSTRUP. Sure.

Secretary CHOLLET. I don't believe so. I think it is—we are not part of that supply line. But we could get back to you with more specifics on how that actually works.

[The information referred to can be found in the Appendix on page 63.]

Dr. WENSTRUP. Sure. Obviously, we have a vested interest in their success and being able to maintain that.

You know, the other question I had—and maybe you can't answer that—but, you know, we have had this dual effort with the space station with the Russians and especially since we have stopped the Space Shuttle.

Where is that in all of this picture going on today, if you have any insight on that?

Secretary CHOLLET. Sir, if we could take that one for the record.

[The information referred to can be found in the Appendix on page 63.]

Dr. WENSTRUP. If you would, I would appreciate it. Thank you. And I have no further questions. I yield back.

Mr. NUGENT. The gentleman yields back.

Mr. Conaway is recognized for 5 minutes.

Mr. CONAWAY. No.

Mr. NUGENT. We appreciate it.

Gentleman, I am going to hold my questions until the classified briefing. But I do appreciate your time that you spent here answering questions for the committee. And with that, we adjourn.

[Whereupon, at 11:51 a.m., the committee was adjourned.]

# APPENDIX

APRIL 8, 2014

PREPARED STATEMENTS SUBMITTED FOR THE RECORD

April 8, 2014

**Opening Statement of Chairman Howard P. "Buck" McKeon**
HEARING ON
**Russian Military Developments and Strategic Implications**
**April 8, 2014**

Good morning ladies and gentlemen. The committee meets to receive testimony on Russian Military Developments and Strategic Implications. Immediately following this hearing, Members will receive a classified briefing by representatives from our intelligence community. Joining us today are Assistant Secretary of Defense for International Security Affairs, Derek Chollet, and Joint Staff Director for Strategic Plans and Policy, Vice Admiral Frank Pandolfe.

Before we get started, I'd like to welcome Congresswoman Tulsi Gabbard to the Committee. Congresswoman Gabbard brings a wealth of experience and unique perspective having served our nation as an enlisted soldier and officer. With Tulsi and Colleen, the service men and women of U.S. Pacific Command and in the great state of Hawaii are well represented. We look forward to working with you.

The events unfolding in Ukraine are deeply troubling: from Russia's invasion and occupation of a sovereign country, to its amassing of tens of thousands of troops along Ukraine's borders and further north under the ruse of conducting "snap exercises." Just this past weekend, we saw reports that Russia is provoking further unrest in eastern Ukraine, attempting to create a reason to invade.

Yet these actions are only the most recent, and perhaps most aggressive, of a broader campaign to challenge the West and to re-establish a Russian sphere of influence in Europe. Mr. Putin is directing a multi-dimensional military modernization effort. Russia is re-arming at an alarming rate with military spending up roughly 30 percent. It stands in flagrant violation of a major nuclear arms control treaty, and under the New START treaty is building up its nuclear forces – by over 100 warheads since the last declaration – while the U.S. reduces its own forces.

As former Secretary of Defense Robert Gates recently wrote in an op-ed, "Mr. Putin… is playing a long game." and that the West must also "play a strategic long game." Yet, the administration's policies have rested largely on reset, cooperation, and further nuclear cuts.

Just last week, Deputy Undersecretary Christine Wormuth testifying on the QDR, stated that they probably would have "added some additional sentences" about Russia given recent developments. That's hardly a re-examination of our nation's policy towards Moscow. And while the QDR states that our military is sized to, and capable of, effectively deterring aggression, there are serious concerns about our ability to do just that – especially with a near peer competitor. Our friends, as well as our adversaries, are watching our every move.  It should come as no surprise that senior Japanese officials raised this issue with Secretary Hagel during his recent visit, as they seek to understand what our policy with regard to Russia's illegal annexation of Crimea signals for our commitments to our allies.

This hearing is an opportunity to examine the strategic implications of Russia's military developments and recent actions. Secretary Chollet and Admiral Pandolfe, I hope you can also discuss how these developments are influencing any re-examination of U.S. policy towards Russia, including our force posture in Europe, how we reassure our allies and partners, and our defense investments.

## Statement of Ranking Member Adam Smith
### HEARING ON
## Russian Military Developments and Strategic Implications
## April 8, 2014

Thank you, Mr. Chairman. And I would also like to thank our witnesses for appearing here today. Admiral Pandolfe, good to see you again. Assistant Secretary Chollet, also a pleasure to see you back here.

Before I get started, I would like to welcome a new member to our committee – Congresswoman Tulsi Gabbard, of Hawaii. Representative Gabbard is filling the seat left by the retirement of our colleague, Rob Andrews. I am sure we all welcome her here and look forward to working with her.

President Putin's recent actions to take control of, and then formally annex, part of the sovereign territory of Ukraine present a direct challenge to the post-Cold War system that we, our European allies, and the members of the former Soviet Union built. The action to illegally seize the territory of another state, by military force, undermines international law, presents a terrible precedent for other nations, and violates Russia's own treaty obligations.

The Administration tried, to its credit, to reach out to Russia and encourage them to participate in this post-Cold War regime. Russia, in Putin's first terms and under then-President Medvedev, even took some halting steps to cooperate with the United States and Europe in building a shared path forward. Some criticized the Administration for this effort, pointing to the 2008 war in Georgia during the last Administration as a reason to not try to engage Russia. But engagement with Russia was always a better course than confrontation, if Russia reciprocated.

Unfortunately, and due solely to the decisions of one man, President Putin, Russia has chosen another course.

I do not believe that Russia will find this course of action to be in their best interests in either the long or the short term. Russia faces uncertain economic prospects with a declining and aging population. Taking actions that lead to greater degrees of economic and diplomatic isolation will not correct this. There are those who believe that Russia's intent was to coerce Ukraine and other former Soviet nations into joining Russia's Eurasian Economic Union rather than the European Union. But seizing Crimea will almost certainly undermine this end—Ukraine possesses the largest economy of any of these countries and would certainly seem to be much less likely to join a Russian-dominated economic union than it was a few months ago.

The Administration has imposed a number of sanctions on Russian and Ukrainian officials and Russian banks, suspended military-to-military contacts, and, with other allies, suspended Russia's membership in the G-8 organization of the most important economies in the world. Europe has taken similar actions. We have also deployed air assets to Europe to assist in patrolling the airspace of our NATO allies and taken a number of other steps to beef up our military presence in Europe.

All of these steps are good. But these steps are not likely to cause Russia to leave Crimea in the near term, if at all. If we are serious about that goal, we are going to have to think seriously, with our European allies, about next steps. Neither I nor any other member here believes that the United States should engage in a military conflict with Russia over the Ukraine. Nor do we want a new Cold War, and, to be clear, I do not believe that is where we are headed. But we do need to make sure that we have postured ourselves to reassure our NATO allies that we will stand with them if required. And we need to think seriously and strategically about the implications of the annexation of Ukrainian territory on the international law regime that we, the Europeans, and many other countries developed to delegitimize wars of conquest. I hope our witnesses can help us with these challenges today.

**Assistant Secretary of Defense Derek Chollet**
**International Security Affairs**
**U.S. Department of Defense**

**House Armed Services Committee**
**"Russian Military Developments and Strategic Implications"**
**April 8, 2014**

Chairman McKeon, Congressman Smith, and Members of the Committee, I appreciate the opportunity to speak to you today on Russia. I will focus my remarks on U.S. policy and actions in the wake of Russia's incursion into Ukraine and continuing threats to Ukraine's sovereignty and territorial integrity, including actions taken by the Department of Defense and with our Allies and international partners.

Russia's unlawful military intervention in Ukraine challenges our vision of a Europe whole, free and at peace. It changes Europe's security landscape. It causes instability on NATO's borders. And it is a challenge to the international order.

Since the outset of the crisis, the United States has pursued three courses of action, consistent with the President's direction to achieve a negotiated, peaceful outcome and to provide President Putin with a diplomatic "off ramp" as an alternative to Russia's use of military force. These courses of action include 1) demonstrating support to Ukraine's transitional government, 2) re-assuring Allies and partners and deterring Russia from further military threats to Europe, and 3) imposing costs on Russia for its illegal actions. The Department of Defense has an important role in achieving U.S. objectives in all three areas.

**Support to Ukraine**

On support to Ukraine, the United States has worked with a range of partners – including the International Monetary Fund (IMF), the United Nations (UN), the European Union (EU), and the Group of 7 (G7) – to help Ukraine through its political transition and economic difficulties, and to demonstrate that the international community stands firmly with the government in Kyiv. The most tangible and powerful sign of support is an $18 billion package from the IMF to restore economic stability. The United States, European Union, and World Bank are providing further economic assistance to complement the IMF program and help Ukraine grow its economy, wean it off dependence on Russia, and move its democracy forward.

For our part, the Department of Defense is working with Ukraine to review, prioritize and grant its defense assistance requests for materials and supplies that would serve to reassure and support Ukraine without taking actions that would escalate the crisis militarily. The first round of this process was completed last week with the delivery of 300,000 Meals Ready-to-Eat to support Ukrainian forces in the field.

In addition, we are maintaining senior-level dialogue with our Ukrainian counterparts, including multiple phone conversations between Secretary of Defense Hagel and the Ukrainian Minister of Defense. Last week, we held bilateral defense consultations in Kyiv, which we moved forward from their original dates in late May 2014. At these consultations, we discussed not only the immediate crisis, but also our mid-term and long-term bilateral defense cooperation. We agreed to work with the Ministry of Defense to continue the effective use of International Military Education and Training (IMET), to review the use of Foreign Military Financing based on Ukraine's new security situation, and to re-evaluate our mutual goals for defense institution building and professional military education in Ukraine. Based on the requirements gleaned from these reviews, we will work with the State Department to identify additional security assistance resources as appropriate.

NATO has reinforced these U.S. actions with Alliance-wide initiatives in support of Ukraine. For example, Allies have offered Ukraine greater access to NATO exercises, invited Ukraine to participate in the development of military capabilities, and offered capacity-building programs for the Ukrainian Armed Forces.

I believe it's important to highlight some important facts about the Ukrainian armed forces. Over the past two months, in this time of adversity, uncertainty, and tremendous political pressure, the armed forces have shown remarkable and commendable professionalism. First, the armed forces did not act against their own citizens during the Maidan protests against the Yanukovych regime. Then, vastly outnumbered by Russian forces in Crimea, they showed courage and dignity. We consider these positive outcomes a direct result of the investments we have made in reform and professionalization of the Ukrainian armed forces, with the support of Congress, over the past two decades.

**Re-assuring Allies and deterring Russia**

The second course of action is re-assuring U.S. Allies and deterring Russia from further military action in Europe. As President Obama said recently in Brussels, the NATO Alliance is "the bedrock of America's security as well as European security."

The United States has taken prompt and high profile steps to re-assure NATO Allies in light of Russia's incursion into Ukraine. Measures so far include augmenting NATO's peacetime Baltic Air Policing mission by deploying 6 additional F-15s to Lithuania. We deployed 12 F-16s and nearly 200 support personnel to Poland to supplement the U.S.-Poland Aviation Detachment training rotation, which was previously scheduled to train with the Polish Air Force. We are also sending three C-130 aircraft to Poland as part of the next scheduled rotation. In March, we extended the USS TRUXTUN's stay in the Black Sea to conduct exercises with Romanian and Bulgarian naval forces, and we will send another U.S. ship to the Black Sea shortly to conduct joint exercises with allies and partners in the region. NATO established orbits of its Airborne Warning and Control System (AWACS) aircraft, over Poland and Romania, both to serve as additional assurance to Allies that border Ukraine and to enhance NATO's situational awareness of activities in the region. The Department of Defense is exploring ways to provide refueling capabilities to the NATO AWACS.

We are also taking measures to support non-NATO security partners who feel directly threatened by Russia's actions. Moldova, for example, has Russian forces on its territory, nominally peacekeepers, but who actually support the separatist Transnistria region. We recently held senior-level consultations with Moldovan officials and discussed options for expanding our Cooperative Threat Reduction programs in that country to help it maintain secure borders. We are also working to address Georgia's concerns through bilateral channels and in the Geneva International discussions, where we continue to focus international attention on Russia's occupation of Georgian territory and work to address the security and humanitarian challenges in areas affected by the conflict.

### Imposing costs on Russia

The third course of action is imposing costs on Russia. Russia's military operation was well planned, executed and resourced by Russian forces from both within Crimea and from Russia itself. Russia's actions require a vigorous, coordinated response, and the United States has led the international community in isolating Russia diplomatically.

The United Nations General Assembly adopted a resolution that affirmed the referendum in Crimea has no validity and cannot alter the status of Crimea. G-7 leaders voiced united support for Ukraine's territorial integrity, called off a planned G-8 Summit hosted by Russia later this year, and expressed willingness to impose coordinated sanctions that will significantly impact Russia's economy, should it continue to escalate the situation in Ukraine. Along with the European Union, Canada, and Australia, we have imposed visa bans and sanctions on a growing list of Russian officials, one Russian bank, and members of Putin's inner circle, along with Ukrainians who played a role in undermining that country's sovereignty or misappropriating Ukrainian assets. The sanctions we have imposed to date are certainly not the end of what we can do.

At the Department of Defense, we have put on hold all military-to-military engagements with Russia, including exercises, bilateral meetings, port visits, and planning conferences. Although we have worked hard over two decades to build a cooperative, transparent defense relationship with Russia, the violations of international law and undermining and stability in Europe mean that we cannot proceed with business as usual. NATO and many Allies have likewise suspended military cooperation and engagements with Russia, while maintaining channels for dialogue that can serve to deescalate the crisis.

And while we do not seek confrontation with Russia, its actions in Europe and Eurasia may require the United States to re-examine our force posture in Europe and our requirement for future deployments, exercises, and training in the region. As Secretary Hagel has said: "The essential character and commitment of (our) alliance... remains unchanged, but we will look for new ways to collaborate and improve the alliance's capabilities and readiness."

**Conclusion**

Mr. Chairman, Congressman Smith, and Members of the Committee, Russia's unlawful actions in Ukraine have dire implications for international and regional security and are a paradigm shift for our relations with Moscow. This crisis is not one generated by the West or the United States. It is a crisis of choice, pursued by Russia to further its interests including its purported annexation of sovereign Ukrainian territory.

I want to conclude by thanking Congress for passing the Support for the Sovereignty, Integrity, Democracy, and Economic Stability of Ukraine Act of 2014. This act is closely aligned with the Administration's objectives, as I've discussed today. It demonstrates solidarity with Ukraine, helps to re-assure our Allies, and imposes further costs on Russia for its actions. Since the stakes are high, and the international principles so fundamental, it is important that the United States speak with one voice during this crisis, and I appreciate that we are doing so.

I look forward to your questions.

### Derek Chollet

### Assistant Secretary of Defense for International Security Affairs

Derek Chollet is the Assistant Secretary of Defense for International Security Affairs (ISA). He is the principal advisor to the Under Secretary of Defense and Secretary of Defense on international security strategy and policy issues related to the nations and international organizations of Europe (including the North Atlantic Treaty Organization), the Middle East, Africa, and the Western Hemisphere. He also has oversight for security cooperation programs, including foreign military sales, in these regions.

Prior to being confirmed in May 2012, Mr. Chollet served at The White House as Special Assistant to the President and Senior Director for Strategic Planning on the National Security Council Staff.

From February 2009 to 2011, Mr. Chollet served in the State Department as the Principal Deputy Director of the Secretary of State's Policy Planning Staff. From November 2008 to January 2009, he was a member of the Obama-Biden Presidential Transition Team.

Previously, Mr. Chollet was a Senior Fellow at The Center for a New American Security (CNAS), a non-resident fellow at the Brookings Institution, and an adjunct associate professor at Georgetown University. During the Clinton Administration he served as Chief Speechwriter for U.S. Ambassador to the United Nations Richard Holbrooke, and as Special Adviser to Deputy Secretary of State Strobe Talbott. From 2002 to 2004, Mr. Chollet was foreign policy adviser to U.S. Senator John Edwards (D-N.C.), both on his legislative staff and during the 2004 Kerry-Edwards presidential campaign.

Mr. Chollet has also been a Fellow at the Center for Strategic and International Studies (CSIS), a Fellow at the American Academy in Berlin, and a visiting scholar and adjunct professor at The George Washington University. He assisted former Secretaries of State James A. Baker III and Warren Christopher with the research and writing of their memoirs, Ambassador Holbrooke with his book on the Dayton peace process in Bosnia, and Deputy Secretary Talbott with his book on U.S.-Russian relations during the 1990s.

Mr. Chollet is the author, co-author or co-editor of six books on American foreign policy, including The Road to the Dayton Accords: A Study of American Statecraft (Palgrave Macmillan, 2005) and America Between the Wars: From 11/9 to 9/11, coauthored with James Goldgeier (PublicAffairs, 2008), and his commentaries and reviews on U.S. foreign policy and politics have appeared in many other books and publications. Raised in Lincoln, Nebraska, Mr. Chollet was educated at Cornell and Columbia.

HOUSE ARMED SERVICES COMMITTEE

OPENING STATEMENT OF

VICE ADMIRAL FRANK C. PANDOLFE, USN

DIRECTOR FOR STRATEGIC PLANS AND POLICY

THE JOINT STAFF

BEFORE THE HOUSE ARMED SERVICES COMMITTEE

8 APRIL 2014

HOUSE ARMED SERVICES COMMITTEE

Chairman McKeon, Ranking Member Smith, and distinguished Committee Members, good morning. Thank you for this opportunity to update you on Russian military developments.

You just heard a review of actions taken by the United States, the NATO Alliance, and the international community in response to Russia's unlawful military intervention in Ukraine. Russia's seizure of Crimea is a flagrant violation of international law, and it reintroduces into Europe the threat of external aggression. By doing so, Russia set back decades of international progress.

The United States military and the wider NATO Alliance have supported our response to this unwarranted intervention:

- We have given support to Ukraine by way of material assistance, defense consultations, and the offer of enhanced training.

- We are reassuring our NATO Allies, with whom we have Article V security guarantees, by sending additional air power to the Baltic States and Poland, increasing our surveillance over Poland and Romania, and sending naval ships into the Black Sea.

- And we are helping to impose costs on Russia by halting all bilateral military-to-military interaction. However, as noted by Mr. Chollet, we are keeping open channels for senior leader communications, to help deescalate the crisis.

I would now like to widen the focus of my remarks beyond Ukraine, to discuss the evolution of Russian conventional military power, thereby providing context to today's events.

At the height of its military power, the Soviet Union was truly a global competitor. With millions of people under arms, vast numbers of tanks and planes, a global navy, and an extensive intelligence gathering infrastructure, the Soviet military machine posed a very real and dangerous threat.

Following the break-up of the Soviet Union in 1991, that arsenal fell into disrepair. Starved of funding and fragmented, Russian military capabilities rapidly decayed throughout the 1990s. From the start of his term in office in 2000, President Putin has made military modernization a top priority of the Russian government. When Russia invaded Georgia in 2008, a number of shortcomings were noted in its military performance. This led the Russian government to further increase investment in its military services.

Since 2008, those efforts have had some success. Russian military forces have been streamlined into smaller, more mobile units. Their overall readiness has improved and their most elite units are well trained and equipped. They now employ a more sophisticated approach to joint warfare.

Their military has implemented organizational change, creating regional commands within Russia. These coordinate and synchronize planning, joint service integration, force movement, intelligence support, and the tactical employment of units.

Finally, the Russian military adopted doctrinal change, placing greater emphasis on speed of movement, the use of Special Operations Forces, and information and cyber warfare. They instituted "snap exercises." These no-notice drills serve the dual purpose of sharpening military readiness while also inducing strategic uncertainty as to whether they will swiftly transition from training to offensive operations.

Today, Russia is a regional power that can project force into nearby states but has very limited global power projection capability. It has a military of uneven readiness. While some units are well trained, most are less so. It suffers from corruption and its logistical capabilities are limited. Aging equipment and infrastructure, fiscal challenges, and demographic and social problems will continue to hamper reform efforts.

The United States, in contrast, employs a military of global reach and engagement. The readiness of our rotationally deployed forces is high and we are working to address readiness shortfalls at home. And we operate within alliances; the strongest of which is NATO. Composed of 28 nations, NATO is the most successful military alliance in history. Should Russia undertake an armed attack against any NATO state, it will find that our commitment to collective defense is immediate and unwavering.

Russia's military objectives are difficult to predict. But it is clear that Russia is sustaining a significant military force on Ukraine's eastern border. This is deeply troubling to all states in the region and beyond, and we are watching Russian military movements very carefully.

I spoke with General Breedlove, the Commander of U.S. European Command and NATO's Supreme Allied Commander, last Friday. He is formulating recommendations for presentation to the North Atlantic Council on April fifteenth. These recommendations will be aimed at further reassuring our NATO allies. As part of this effort, he will consider increasing military exercises, forward deploying additional military equipment and personnel, and increasing our naval, air, and ground presence. He will update members of Congress on those recommendations at the earliest opportunity.

Ladies and gentlemen, thank you for this opportunity to address your Committee. I look forward to your questions.

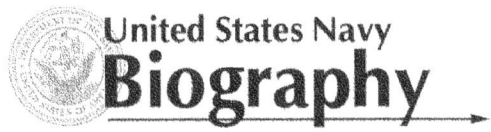

# United States Navy
# Biography

## Vice Admiral Frank Craig Pandolfe
### DIRECTOR FOR STRATEGIC PLANS AND POLICY
### JOINT STAFF, J-5

Vice Adm. Pandolfe is the Director for Strategic Plans and Policy (J-5), Joint Staff, the Pentagon, Washington, D.C. He provides strategic direction, policy guidance, and planning focus enabling the Chairman of the Joints Chiefs of Staff to provide best military advice to the President, the Secretary of Defense and the National Security Council. He assumed those duties Dec. 4, 2013.

He grew up in New England, graduated with distinction from the U.S. Naval Academy in 1980, and was awarded a doctorate in International Relations from the Fletcher School of Law and Diplomacy at Tufts University in 1987.

At-sea, he served in USS David R. Ray (DD 971), USS John Hancock (DD 981), USS Hue City (CG 66), and USS Forrestal (CV 59). He commanded USS Mitscher (DDG 57) from 1999 to 2001, earning three Battle Efficiency Awards for operational excellence and three Golden Anchor awards for superior retention. He subsequently commanded Destroyer Squadron 18 from 2003 to 2004, operating as sea combat commander for Enterprise Carrier Strike Group in support of Operation Iraqi Freedom. From 2008 to 2009, he led Theodore Roosevelt Carrier Strike Group on a combat deployment in support of Operation Enduring Freedom in Afghanistan.

Ashore, he was assigned to the Navy Staff as executive assistant to the Chief of Naval Operations, the Joint Staff as the Deputy Director for Joint Strategic Planning, and the White House Staff as military aide and advisor to the Vice President of the United States, and Director, Surface Warfare Division, OPNAV N86. Most recently, he served as the Commander, 6th Fleet and, Striking and Support Forces NATO.

Pandolfe's personal decorations include the Defense Superior Service Medal, Legion of Merit, Meritorious Service Medal, and additional individual, campaign, and unit awards.

Updated: 3 January 2014

# DOCUMENTS SUBMITTED FOR THE RECORD

APRIL 8, 2014

# The Washington Post

Back to previous page

## John Kerry's departure from reality

**By Jackson Diehl, Published: March 30**

During a tour of the Middle East in November, Secretary of State John F. Kerry portrayed the region as on its way to a stunning series of breakthroughs, thanks to U.S. diplomacy. In Egypt, he said, "the roadmap" to democracy "is being carried out, to the best of our perception." In Syria, a peace conference would soon replace the Assad regime with a transitional government, because "the Russians and the Iranians . . . will make certain that the Syrian regime will live up to its obligation."

Last but hardly least, the Israeli-Palestinian conflict was on its way to a final settlement — by April. "This is not mission impossible," insisted the secretary of state. "This can happen."

Some people heaped praise on Kerry for his bold ambitions, saying he was injecting vision and energy into the Obama administration's inert foreign policy. Others, including me, said he was delusional.

Four months have passed, and, sadly for Kerry and U.S. interests, the verdict is in: delusional. Egypt is under the thumb of an authoritarian general. The Syrian peace talks imploded soon after they began. Kerry is now frantically trying to prevent the collapse of the Israeli-Palestinian negotiations, which are hanging by a thread — and all sides agree there will be no deal in April.

It might be argued that none of this is Kerry's fault. It was Gen. Abdel Fatah al-Sissi who hijacked Egypt's promised political transition. It was the Assad regime that refused to negotiate its departure . It was Benjamin Netanyahu who kept building Jewish settlements in the West Bank. It was Mahmoud Abbas who refused to recognize Israel as a Jewish state.

All true; and yet all along the way, Kerry — thanks to a profound misreading of the realities on the ground — was enabling the bad guys.

Start with Egypt. Since last summer the State Department and its chief have been publicly endorsing the fiction that the military coup against the elected government of Mohamed Morsi was aimed at "restoring democracy," as Kerry put it. As late as March 12, Kerry — spun by his friend Nabil Fahmy, the regime's slick foreign minister — declared that "I'm very, very hopeful that, in very short order, we'll be able to move forward" in certifying that Egypt was eligible for a full resumption of U.S. aid.

Twelve days later, an Egyptian court handed death sentences to 529 members of the Muslim Brotherhood after a two-day trial. Two days after that, Sissi appeared on television, in uniform, to announce that he would "run" for president.

Kerry was no less credulous of Vladimir Putin. Having taken office with the intention of boosting support for Syrian rebels as a way of "changing Assad's calculations," Kerry abruptly changed course last May after a visit to the Kremlin. Russia and the United States, he announced, would henceforth "cooperate in trying to implement" a transition from the Assad regime. "Our understanding," Mr. Kerry said of himself and Putin, "is very similar."

Only it wasn't. Putin, who loathes nothing more than U.S.-engineered regime change, spent the next nine months pouring weapons into Damascus, even as Kerry continued to insist that Moscow would force Assad to hand over power in Geneva. When the Geneva conference finally convened, Russia — to the surprise of virtually no one, other than Kerry — backed Assad's contention that the negotiations should be about combating "terrorism," not a transitional government.

That brings us to the Israeli-Palestinian quagmire, which Kerry made his personal cause even though the Obama administration already had tried and abjectly failed to broker a deal between Netanyahu and Abbas and Israel and the Palestinian territories are currently an island of tranquility in a blood-drenched Middle East. Ignoring the counsel of numerous experts who warned neither side was ready for a deal, Kerry lavished time on the two men, convinced that his political skills would bring them around.

Predictably, that didn't happen. The leaders have not budged a millimeter from the positions they occupied on Palestinian statehood a year ago, and Abbas has been strident in publicly rejecting terms Kerry tried to include in a proposed peace "framework."

Kerry offered an answer to my first critique of him in an interview with Susan Glasser of Politico: "I would ask" anyone "who was critical of our engagement: What is the alternative?" Well, the alternative is to address the Middle East as it really is. Recognize that Egypt's generals are reinstalling a dictatorship and that U.S. aid therefore cannot be resumed; refocus on resuscitating and defending Egypt's real democrats. Admit that the Assad regime won't quit unless it is defeated on the battlefield and adopt a strategy to bring about that defeat. Concede that a comprehensive Israeli-Palestinian peace isn't possible now and look for more modest ways to build the groundwork for a future Palestinian state.

In short, drop the delusions.

*Read more from Jackson Diehl's archive, follow him on Twitter or subscribe to his updates on Facebook.*

Read more about this issue: Jackson Diehl: John Kerry's Middle East dream world The Post's View: John Kerry's empty words on Syria David Ignatius: John Kerry, a secretary on a mission The Post's View: Will John Kerry's Mideast peace framework bring results? The Post's View: Mr. Kerry's diplomatic games in Egypt

# WITNESS RESPONSES TO QUESTIONS ASKED DURING THE HEARING

## APRIL 8, 2014

## RESPONSES TO QUESTIONS SUBMITTED BY DR. WENSTRUP

Secretary CHOLLET. NASA and Roscosmos will continue to work together to maintain the safe and continuous operation of the International Space Station (ISS), where humans have lived continuously for more than 13 years. The success of the ISS program depends on the mutual dependence of all partners, and reflects the unique contributions each partner provides in support of the program. We believe that it is in the interest of all the ISS partners to continue our normal operational and programmatic cooperation, and not to allow disruption of any of the activities that have maintained a continuous human presence on orbit for more than a decade. I defer additional questions regarding the ISS to NASA. [See page 36.]

Secretary CHOLLET. Sir, I agree with you that we have a vested interest in the success of the Afghan National Security Forces (ANSF); the rotary-wing capability we are building for them around the Mi-17 helicopter is critical to this success.

Because the Department of Defense (DOD) is investing a substantial amount of Afghanistan Security Forces Funds and DOD counternarcotics funds in the procurement and sustainment of the Afghan fleet, DOD asked the Department of the Army to establish the Project Manager-Non-Standard Rotary-Wing Aircraft (PM–NSRWA) under Program Executive Office-Aviation in 2010. PM–NSRWA serves as the life-cycle manager for Afghanistan's Mi-17s and is our lead entity for interfacing with the Mi-17 supply line.

Because the Mi-17 is a Russian-made helicopter, the manufacturing is performed in Russia and the parts supply line originates predominantly with Russian companies. For procurements of new aircraft, PM–NSRWA contracts with Rosoboronexport (ROE) rather than the manufacturer because we are buying military variants, and Russian defense exports must go through ROE. For maintenance, spare parts procurement, and overhauls of the Mi-17s, PM–NSRWA contracts with U.S. companies, which then use subcontractors to buy spare parts mainly from the Russian manufacturers to ensure they obtain certified parts and to perform overhauls at Russian-certified overhaul facilities.

Using Russian-certified parts and overhaul facilities is important to maintaining official Russian airworthiness certification of the aircraft, which ensures that our air advisors—who are crucial to developing Afghan aviation capability—are flying on well-maintained aircraft. To support airworthiness certification of the aircraft, PM–NSRWA also contracts with the Mi-17 manufacturer for engineering services to ensure the manufacturer has cognizance of the aircraft. PM–NSRWA also contracts for technical bulletins about the aircraft. [See page 36.]

www.ingramcontent.com/pod-product-compliance
Lightning Source LLC
Chambersburg PA
CBHW080535290526
45790CB00006B/2419